FIVE THOUSAND YEARS OF
Slavery

MARJORIE GANN and JANET WILLEN

TUNDRA BOOKS

Published in the United States by Tundra Books of Northern New York,
P.O. Box 1030, Plattsburgh, New York 12901

Library of Congress Control Number: 2009938446

Library and Archives Canada Cataloguing in Publication

Gann, Marjorie
Five thousand years of slavery / Marjorie Gann, Janet Willen.

Includes index.
ISBN 978-0-88776-914-6

1. Slavery – History – Juvenile literature.
I. Willen, Janet II. Title.

HT861.G35 2011   j306.3'6209   C2009-905868-5

We acknowledge the financial support of the Government of Canada
through the Book Publishing Industry Development Program
(BPIDP) and that of the Government of Ontario through the Ontario
Media Development Corporation's Ontario Book Initiative. We
further acknowledge the support of the Canada Council for the Arts
and the Ontario Arts Council for our publishing program.

ONTARIO ARTS COUNCIL
CONSEIL DES ARTS DE L'ONTARIO

Design: Leah Springate

Printed and bound in China

1 2 3 4 5 6   16 15 14 13 12 11

This book is dedicated to the memory of our parents, Aaron and Alice Lowenstein,
who taught us by example that all people are created equal.

AUTHORS' NOTE

For historical accuracy, we have kept the original spelling, punctuation, and capitalization of the people we quoted unless we needed to make a slight change for clarity. Sometimes we have also included comments by people who used words or sentiments that are offensive to us. Obnoxious as they are, these statements reveal to us the racial prejudices used to justify slavery.

Many place names have changed through the years. Depending on the context, we either replaced the earlier name with today's or indicated the modern name in brackets. Place names in the maps correspond to those in the text, and so the maps do not match a specific period of time.

ACKNOWLEDGMENTS

We are grateful to the many scholars and antislavery experts who helped us to understand how slavery worked in the past and how it operates today. First and foremost, our thanks go to Professor Martin Klein of the University of Toronto, whose extensive knowledge of world slavery guided our research and who generously read and commented on our manuscript. Kevin Bales, president and co-founder of Free the Slaves, gave us an expert's insight into the complexity of modern slavery. Thanks, too, to Professor Lara Braitstein, McGill University, Montreal, for her assistance with understanding Buddhism; to Natalie Zemon Davis, professor of history emeritus from Princeton University and currently associated with the University of Toronto, for opening our eyes to John Gabriel Stedman's account of the slave Quassie; to Andres Dobat, PhD, Aarhus University, for reading the sections on the Vikings; to Muriel Guigue of the International Cocoa Initiative, Stephanie Mannone of Free the Children, and Laura Germino, of the Coalition of Immokalee Workers, for checking the material relating to their organizations for accuracy; to Rabbi Edward Elkin, First Narayever Congregation, Toronto, for helping us to contextualize biblical law and Hebrew practice; to Kent Hackmann, professor emeritus, University of Idaho, for reviewing the chapter on South America and the Caribbean; to Randy J. Sparks, professor and chair, Department of History, Tulane University, and author of *The Two Princes of Calabar: An Eighteenth-Century Odyssey*, for answering our questions about the Robin Johns; to Professor Ehud R. Toledano, Holder, University Chair for Ottoman Studies, Department of Middle East and African History, Tel Aviv University, for his helpful suggestions on Ottoman slavery; to James F. Warren, professor, Southeast Asian Modern History, Murdoch University, and author of *Iranun and Balangingi: Globalization, Maritime Raiding and the Birth of Ethnicity*, for guiding us through the Sulu Zone; and to Marcia Wright, professor of history (emerita), Columbia University, New York, and author of *Strategies of Slaves & Women: Life-stories from East/Central Africa*, for helping to place the stories of Msatulwa Mwachitete and Meli in their cultural and historical context, and Terence Walz of Lilian Barber Press for granting us permission to print excerpts from these narratives. Of course, any errors or misinterpretations are entirely our own.

Special thanks are due Francis Buk, who arrived in the United States with a forged Sudanese passport that incorrectly spelled his name Bok, and reclaimed his parents' name when he became a U.S. citizen in 2007. Buk generously shared the story of his enslavement and escape with us. We hope that his experiences, as told here and in his memoir, *Escape from Slavery*, will inspire our readers to join the fight to wipe slavery off the face of the earth.

Our thanks to the people at Tundra Books – to Kathy Lowinger, who saw the potential in our proposal and helped to shape our ideas into a readable story; to Kathryn Cole, who remained unflappable despite the book's inevitable birth pangs; to Lauren Campbell, who chased down permissions for many elusive images; and to Gena Gorrell, whose eagle eye spotted things we would surely have missed.

Our love and thanks to our families – Mark, Andy, Deborah, Eleanore, and Joey – for their support and encouragement, and to the many friends who lent us books, referred us to websites, sent us articles, and lifted our spirits.

Finally, we are grateful to all those slaves who bravely told their stories so their plight would not be forgotten.

CONTENTS

TO BE A SLAVE   1

1   KINGS, PHARAOHS, AND PROPHETS   3
The Ancient Near East

2   REBELLION AND REVENGE   11
Ancient Greece and Rome

3   SAINTS AND VIKINGS   21
Europe in the Middle Ages

4   IN THE REALM OF THE QUR'AN   32
Slavery under Islam

5   CARAVANS, CANOES, AND CAPTIVES   42
Africa

6   EXPLORERS, LABORERS, WARRIORS, CHIEFS   52
The Americas

7   THE TREACHEROUS TRIANGLE   61
South America and the Caribbean

8   "THE MONSTER IS DEAD!"   78
British Abolition

9   IN THE LAND OF LIBERTY   94
North America

10   CIVIL WAR, CIVIL RIGHTS   111
The United States

11   BLACKBIRDERS, COOLIES, AND SLAVE GIRLS   129
Asia and the Southern Pacific

12   SLAVERY IS NOT HISTORY   144
The Modern World

TO BE FREE   157

Time Line   160
Sources   162
Index   164

"If slavery is not wrong, nothing is wrong."
– *U.S. President Abraham Lincoln, April 4, 1864*

TO BE A SLAVE

Francis felt honored and excited. His mother was sending him to the marketplace to sell hard-cooked eggs and peanuts, with only the older village children to watch out for him. Francis was just seven years old, but he knew his mother was giving him a big responsibility. He was determined to make her proud. She handed a bigger boy the buckets of food to carry, but Francis took them from him. *If I am big enough to go to the market without my parents*, he thought, *I am strong enough to carry two pails.*

The market was crowded, and pungent odors of fresh meat and fish, fruits, vegetables, and tobacco filled the air. People were chattering and bargaining and joking. Suddenly the mood changed. Smoke began rising from a nearby village. Sellers hastily packed up their goods. Before Francis and the other children could decide what to do, men on horseback galloped into the marketplace, their firearms blasting and their swords slashing. Everyone was terrified.

By the time the attack was over, the sun was setting. A man grabbed Francis, dropped him into a basket tied to a donkey's back, and rode off with him. When they finally stopped at a clearing, Francis recognized children from the marketplace, crying and clinging to each other. Another man, big and bearded, hoisted Francis onto his horse and set out into the night. Francis was terrified and confused. Where were they going? Who was this man?

Francis found out when they reached a farm. The man, Giemma, was greeted by his wife. The couple watched and laughed as their children, by way of welcome, beat Francis with sticks until his skin burned.

Francis had become Giemma's slave. His new master put the boy to work as a cowherd. Sometimes when Francis was in the forest with the cattle, Giemma sent armed riders to spy on him. If they reported that the child had done something wrong, Giemma would beat him.

At first Francis could not speak Giemma's language, but he listened carefully so that he could learn. One day he was able to ask Giemma a question: "Why does no one love me?" Giemma did not answer. Francis tried again. "Why do you make me sleep with the animals?" For two days Giemma said nothing, but then he replied, "Because you *are* an animal."

The years went by, and Francis grew up without a kind word or gesture. "I'd been longing to see someone . . . come one day and give me a smile and actually say 'hello' or 'How did you sleep last night?'" he explained later, "but I never heard such things."

But he did remember how his father had called him *muycharko*, which means "twelve men," because even as a small boy he had worked hard. "He said when I am a grownup, I will do something that twelve men can do." He consoled himself by thinking of his mother's kindness. "When you're alone, you're not really alone, because God is watching you," she had told him.

Slavery – ownership or absolute control of one person by another – has been the fate of millions of people like Francis for over five thousand years. In this book you'll read about warrior kings who boasted of the captives they brought home from battle to build lavish royal palaces, and about a humble Egyptian shepherd who rented out his slave girl in exchange for some new clothes. You will read about the slaves who died in silver mines in Ancient Greece, and others who organized revolts in Ancient Rome. You'll read Viking poems that describe slaves as ugly, deformed creatures, and hear of a rebellious slave in Renaissance Italy who had her nose and lips cut off. From medieval Arab travelers you'll learn about slave raids in Africa before Europeans arrived there. The accounts of European explorers will tell you how some Native Americans were forced into slavery, and how others sacrificed slaves to their gods. Former slaves will describe what it was like to cross the ocean in a slave ship in the 1700s, and slave owners will explain how they managed the slaves on their sugar plantations.

Much has been written about the abolition of slavery in the Americas, but we know a lot less about slavery in the world we live in today. Today's freed slaves – who have worked everywhere from factories in China, to farms in Sudan, to tomato fields in Florida – tell of the tricks used to lure them away from their homes and families, and their miserable working conditions and mistreatment.

Slavery is in some ways always the same, whenever and wherever it is practiced. It wrenches people away from everything dear to them – homeland, language, family, and friends. It strips them of the right to choose their work, their amusements, their friends, their clothes, and sometimes even their names. Above all, it denies the fact that every human being has feelings of love and a need to be loved. If we are to put an end to slavery in the world we live in, the first step is to learn about it.

CHAPTER 1
KINGS, PHARAOHS, AND PROPHETS: THE ANCIENT NEAR EAST

Some say that the oldest story ever written down is the Sumerian epic of *Gilgamesh*, a four-thousand-year-old tale of gods, kings, love, and slavery.

> He is king, he does whatever he wants,
> takes the son from his father and crushes him,
> takes the girl from her mother and uses her,
> the warrior's daughter, the young man's bride,
> he uses her, no one dares to oppose him.

Even in this ancient tale, the people cry out against slavery:

> Heavenly Father, Gilgamesh – noble
> as he is, splendid as he is –
> has exceeded all bounds.
> The people suffer from his
> Tyranny, the people cry out . . .
> Father, *do* something, quickly before the people
> Overwhelm heaven with their heartrending cries.

We don't know what work the sons and daughters were forced to do, but we know that they suffered.

What is it like to be a slave, to have no control over what happens to your body, how you spend your time, where you live, or whom you live with? The answer depends on where slavery is practiced and who is practicing it. But whatever form it takes – and there are many forms – slavery has been woven into our history since the earliest times.

Slavery was part of life in Mesopotamia, the region we now call Iraq, where our recorded history begins. For over 1,500 years, Mesopotamia saw the rise and fall of mighty kingdoms: first Sumer and Akkad, and later Assyria in the north and

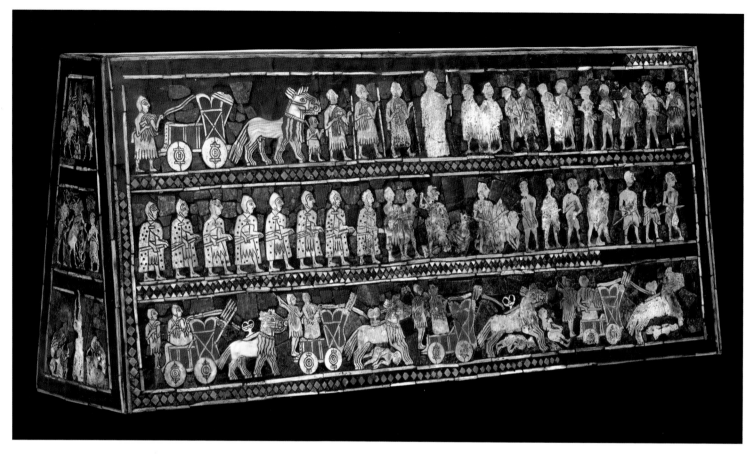

This Sumerian panel, known as the Standard of Ur, was discovered in the Royal Cemetery in the ancient city of Ur. It shows a victorious army marching its captive soldiers naked to the king, who holds a spear. Notice the elegant chariots.

Babylonia in the south. The kingdoms were powerful, their rulers were warlike, and they built their empires on the backs of slaves.

The Sumerian kings brought home more and more foreign captives to work in their palace workshops, and even as soldiers in their armies. Although Sumer disappeared thousands of years ago, the long lists of male and female war captives survive, carved on clay tablets.

The Great Empires of Assyria and Babylonia

Centuries passed, and Sumer and Akkad gave way to the empires of Assyria and Babylonia. Like the others before them, they went to war often, and when they did, they brought back captives. Soon they had huge slave workforces. The cruel Assyrian king Ashurnasirpal II advertised his brutality on large carved tablets. After

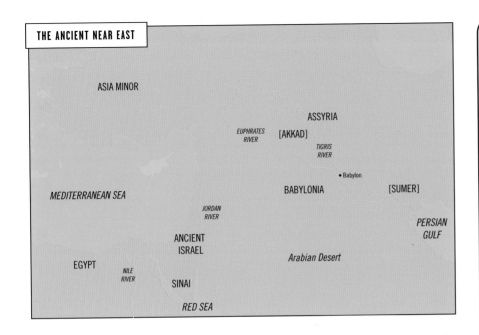

THE ANCIENT NEAR EAST

ASIA MINOR

ASSYRIA

EUPHRATES RIVER [AKKAD]

TIGRIS RIVER

• Babylon

MEDITERRANEAN SEA BABYLONIA [SUMER]

JORDAN RIVER

PERSIAN GULF

ANCIENT ISRAEL

Arabian Desert

EGYPT

NILE RIVER

SINAI

RED SEA

one expedition he bragged that he was returning from war with 460 horses, 2,000 cattle, 5,000 sheep, the sister of the defeated ruler, and the daughters of the ruler's rich nobles, as well as 15,000 other people.

These captives built the Assyrians' legendary city, Nimrud, with its five-mile (8-km) wall, grand palace, botanical gardens, and zoo. But slaves were not just laborers in Assyria; some were musicians, domestic servants, temple or library workers, sailors and soldiers for the annual spring military campaigns, charioteers, or grooms for the cavalry's horses. Slaves even worked as healers and as scholars. By the end of the Assyrian Empire, slave markets were dotted around the Mediterranean Sea and the Persian Gulf.

Just as people have taken one another as slaves from the earliest times, history also shows us that people have risked everything to escape slavery. Babylonian accounts tell of slave uprisings and runaway slaves and owners who did whatever they could to hold onto their "property": they made their slaves wear clay or metal tablets on chains, or burned their names or symbols into the flesh of their slaves.

THE CODE OF KING HAMMURABI OF BABYLON

"If a man has stolen a child, he shall be put to death."

This anti-kidnapping law can be found in one of the earliest and most complete legal codes of ancient times — the Code of Hammurabi. As ruler of the city-state of Babylon, Hammurabi brought many of the surrounding city-states under his power. He had this code of law carved into a black stone pillar taller than a man, so all his subjects could see it.

If a physician heal[s] the broken bone or diseased soft part of a man, the patient shall pay the physician five shekels in money. . . . If he is a slave his owner shall pay the physician two shekels.

Laws like these limited the owner's power over his slave. He could not get away with killing a rebellious slave — all he could do was cut off his ear. This may have had less to do with the sanctity of the slave's life than with the value of the slave to society. For the same reason, helping a slave to escape, or protecting a runaway slave, was punishable by death.

Egypt, Land of the Pharaohs

In the early years of Egyptian history – what is known as the Old Kingdom – a form of forced labor called corvée was practiced. The pharaoh owned all the land, so every person who farmed it was his tenant. When the pharaoh's tenants weren't needed on farms, they had to work on construction projects in exchange for food and clothing. These were the workers who built the magnificent pyramids. Though they had little choice about the work they did, they weren't slaves – they could own their own homes and, most important, nobody could sell them.

But as time went on, the line between free and forced work was more sharply drawn. A laborer who tried to escape his corvée work could be punished with enslavement, together with his whole family. Though this document is thousands of years old, it is still chilling:

> Order issued by the Great Prison in year 31, third month of the summer season, day 5, that he be condemned with all his family to labor for life on state land, according to the decision of the court.

Foreign Slaves

Like the empires that went before, Egypt had a growing appetite for war, and with each victory soldiers brought home foreign captives to become slaves. One warrior boasted:

> I have brought back in great numbers those that my sword has spared, with their hands tied behind their backs before my horses, and their wives and children in tens of thousands, and their livestock in hundreds of thousands. I have imprisoned their leaders in fortresses bearing my name, and I have added to them chief archers and tribal chiefs, branded and enslaved, tattooed with my name, and their wives and children have been treated in the same way.

War was not the only way Egyptians got their slaves. Like the Assyrians and Babylonians, they bought impoverished people who were in debt. They also bought slaves, along with dates and spices, from the nomadic traders who led caravans across the desert.

Eventually almost anybody could afford to own a slave. People would even rent

The head on this fragment from a stone carving tells us that Egyptian armies brought back African captives as slaves. The carving is almost 2,500 years old.

out their slaves to earn a bit of money. In one early document we read about a shepherd who complains that he needs clothes; he offers another shepherd two days of his slave's work in exchange for garments.

Not only was slavery common, but the Egyptians feared they might be enslaved even after they died. They believed that life after death would be much like life on earth, and they placed in their tombs statuettes of wood and pottery representing workers who would do the jobs of slaves after death.

By about 2,400 years ago, Egypt was no longer a great power. Slavery dwindled with the empire.

Slavery in Ancient Israel

Like their neighbors, the Hebrews kept slaves. The Bible introduces several slaves by name, and describes them as part of the family. Abraham, the first Jew, has a wife named Sarah and a son named Isaac. Sarah has an Egyptian slave, Hagar, and Abraham is the father of Hagar's son, Ishmael. Fearing that Ishmael will share her son Isaac's inheritance, Sarah has him and his mother sent off into the wilderness,

FROM ADOPTION TO FREEDOM

Some slaves in Ancient Egypt were lucky enough to be adopted by their owners. In a document known as the Adoption Papyrus, we learn how one mistress adopted and then freed her slave's children:

We bought the slave girl Dienihatiri, and she gave birth to three children, a boy and two girls, three in all. And I adopted, fed, and raised them, and to this day they have never treated me badly. On the contrary, they have treated me well, and I have no sons or daughters other than them. And the overseer of the stables, Pendiu, connected to me by family ties, since he is my younger brother, came into my house and took the elder sister, Taimennut, as his wife. And I accepted this on her behalf and he is now with her. Now, I have freed her, and if she gives birth to a son or daughter, they too will be free citizens in the land of the Pharaoh. . . .

7

In the Bible story, God sends an angel to comfort Sarah's slave, Hagar, when she and her son are alone and desperate in the desert.

with only a loaf of bread and a waterskin. Soon their food is gone and, worse, so is their water. Hagar is a devoted mother who feels powerless to save her child. But God hears her cries and, slaves or not, saves them.

As new generations appear in the Bible, so does the story of slavery. Joseph, Abraham's great-grandson, is sold by his jealous brothers into slavery in Egypt. When he is promoted to a high position in the pharaoh's court, he rescues the Egyptians from famine. Generations later, under a new pharaoh who does not remember Joseph, the Hebrews are enslaved by the Egyptians.

The pharaoh decides that the Hebrews are becoming a threat to his power and orders that every newborn Hebrew baby be killed. But the mother of one baby, Moses, places him in a basket in the Nile River. An Egyptian princess rescues him and decides to raise him in the palace. When Moses grows up and sees how his people suffer as slaves, he is angered. God chooses him to approach the pharaoh with the words "Let my people go." Again and again, the pharaoh refuses. Finally God frees the Hebrews, parting the waters of the sea so they can begin their long march to freedom.

This event, the Exodus, is the central story of the Hebrew Bible. Later, when God gives the Israelites the Ten Commandments in the desert, He reminds them that they were slaves in Egypt:

Six days you shall labor and do all your work, but the seventh day is a Sabbath of the Lord your God: you shall not do any work – you, your son or daughter, your male or female slave, your ox or your ass, or any of your cattle, or the stranger in your settlements, so that your male and female slave may rest as you do. Remember that you were a slave in the land of Egypt and the Lord your God freed you from there.

Slavery Laws in the Bible

Over and over in the Bible, God reminds the Israelites that they were once slaves. By recalling their own bitter lives, they may understand what it feels like to be oppressed, and learn to treat the poor and downtrodden with loving-kindness.

The Hebrews' neighbors had harsh laws that instructed slave owners to cut off the nose and ears of a slave who did not obey, or to scour out the mouth of an insolent slave with a quart of salt. According to the Hebrew Bible, however, slaves are human beings, not just property. They must not be mistreated. "When a man strikes the eye of his slave, male or female, and destroys it, he shall let him go free on account of his eye. If he knocks out the tooth of his slave, male or female, he shall let him go free on account of his tooth." A master may not kill a slave, and taking captives to enslave or sell is forbidden.

The law did nonetheless favor the *Hebrew* slave, who had presumably sold himself to repay a debt. Such debt bondage was not permanent: "If a fellow Hebrew, man or woman, is sold to you, he shall serve you six years, and in the seventh year you shall set him free." Although foreign slaves could be slaves forever, the Bible forbids turning over a runaway slave, Hebrew or not, to his master: "He shall live with you in any place he may choose among the settlements in your midst, where he pleases; you must not ill-treat him."

Slavery in Real Life

We know what biblical law said, but we don't know how slaves were actually treated. We do know that biblical prophets scolded the people for ignoring the ideals of the Bible. One prophet asks, What good is

Every year at Passover, Jewish people read from the *Haggadah*, a book that tells the story of their escape from slavery in Egypt. This fourteenth-century illustration shows Hebrew slaves lifting heavy loads to the top of a tower as they build a city for the Egyptian pharaoh.

THE FIRST ABOLITIONISTS

Two Jewish sects' way of living placed them at odds with the entire slave-owning ancient world.

The Essenes did not have slaves, and they condemned slavery, and the Therapeutae considered that the ownership of servants was against nature. The Essenes and Therapeutae weren't typical for the times. It took many centuries before any other abolitionists came along.

it to try to be pious by carrying out rituals like fasting if you fail to free the oppressed?

> No, this is the fast I desire:
> To unlock the fetters of wickedness,
> And untie the cords of the yoke
> To let the oppressed go free;
> To break every yoke.

These ancient words would inspire those who fought slavery thousands of years later.

CHAPTER 2
REBELLION AND REVENGE: ANCIENT GREECE AND ROME

In the year 73 BCE, in Capua, Italy, a desperate group of seventy slaves armed only with kitchen knives escaped their masters and fled to the crater of Mount Vesuvius.

These were no ordinary slaves. They were Roman gladiators – skilled entertainers who were forced to fight to the death in front of thousands of people in open-air arenas. A fortunate few achieved such glory in the ring that they earned fame, lavish gifts, and, most important, their freedom. Most gladiators died a painful and humiliating death as spectators cheered.

These gladiators were joined by forty thousand ragtag outlaws, outcasts, and runaway slaves. They followed a leader whose name has come down to us through

Roman gladiators sometimes had to fight wild animals like lions or bears in the arena. In this mosaic, the gladiator is pitted against leopards.

NOW SHOWING IN THE ARENA!
Part showman, part athlete, all slave. That was a gladiator.

Gladiators had the most dangerous job of any slave entertainers. They had to kill or be killed. Depending on their training, they could use various weapons – shield and sword, dagger and buckler (small shield), slingshot, net and trident (triple spear), or short sword – and they could fight on foot or horseback, or even in chariots. Opponents usually did not use the same weapons; a man with a net might try to entangle a heavily armed opponent and then stab him with a trident. In some spectacles, men even fought elephants or other animals.

(continued)

Each bout was a life-or-death struggle. Sometimes, as soon as one gladiator died, another stepped in to do battle. At some games, no contestant was allowed to survive. At others, if one of the gladiators was so badly wounded that he could no longer fight, he would lie on his back and raise his left hand. The victor would turn to the emperor, sponsor, or spectators to decide the wounded man's fate. By waving handkerchiefs or using hand gestures equivalent to our "thumbs up" or "thumbs down," these judges would show whether they thought the fighter had been brave and should live, or had been disappointing — in which case the victorious opponent would kill him.

The winner couldn't rejoice for long. He would receive expensive gifts but would still have to fight again. The very best gladiators might win a wooden sword to show that they had won their freedom, but that hardly ever happened. Brutal as they were, these displays were so popular that by the fourth century CE they were taking place 175 days a year in Rome.

This shows one version of the death of Spartacus. The heroic slave proved his devotion to his rebel army by killing his own horse, saying that the enemy had plenty of good horses he could use if he won — and if he lost, he wouldn't need a horse. As it turned out, he didn't need one.

history — Spartacus. In his own day Spartacus was notorious as a rebel. Today he is remembered as a hero for his fight for freedom.

Spartacus had been a member of a Roman legion, an infantry unit in the army, but he had deserted and been captured and sold into slavery. When his skill as a fighter caught his captors' eye, he was trained to be a gladiator. After Spartacus and the runaways fled to Mount Vesuvius, the government of Rome mustered its forces to quash them. Perhaps the government thought it would be easy to put down a rebellion of poorly armed slaves and outcasts, or perhaps they didn't have a large enough army to go against the rebels — there were two other wars going on at the time. Whatever the reason, Spartacus and his supporters outsmarted and outfought the Romans for months.

When the Roman army first came to Mount Vesuvius, the commander stationed his men along the only passable road from the mountaintop and waited for the rebels to come down. But while the Romans were waiting, Spartacus and his men crafted ladders out of wild vines and used them to climb down another side of the mountain. They launched a surprise attack on the Romans from behind. The slaves won that battle and many more battles to come, until the army returned to Rome in disgrace.

But eventually the Roman troops proved too much for Spartacus. The Romans killed most of the rebels in battle but saved six thousand of them for crucifixion. They nailed them to wooden crosses lining the road from Capua to Rome to warn other slaves of the horrible fate awaiting them if they dared to challenge the authorities. No one knows whether Spartacus fell in battle or suffered a slow death on a cross.

Falling into Slavery

If you had lived in Ancient Greece or Rome from about 800 BCE to 500 CE, you almost certainly would have been either a slave or a slave owner, because slaves were such a common part of everyday life. We don't know how many slaves lived in Greece, but historians estimate that by the end of the first century BCE, two million of the six million people in Roman Italy were slaves.

In the early days of Ancient Greece, slaves and masters lived and worked side by side. There was no question that the masters had power of life and death over their slaves, but everyday life was not as bleak for them as it would become in later years.

The Romans conquered Greece and kept spreading their power until they dominated Europe. At its height, the Roman Empire extended as far west as today's France, Spain, and England, as far east as Albania, and along the northern shore of Africa.

During their conquests, both Greek and Roman soldiers traveled from land to land by sea, foot, or horse, claiming newly conquered territories as their own and enslaving those they defeated along the way. "It is a law established for all time among all men that when a city is taken in war, the persons and the property of its inhabitants belong to the captors," wrote one Greek historian.

THE MIGHTY SPARTANS

Like most conquerors, the Greeks who lived in the city-state of Sparta enslaved those they vanquished. But they did not sell their captives in a marketplace to be transported far away. Instead, they enslaved them right in their own towns. One of the first towns they enslaved was Helos, in southern Greece; the word "helot" has come to mean any slave or serf. The Spartans forced the Helots to work land around Helos, to give a portion of the food they produced to Spartan families, and to follow the Spartans to war as servants. Although the Spartans were the masters, they were outnumbered by the Helots, so they lived in constant fear that their slaves would plot against them and revolt. Every year or so, the Spartans killed a prominent Helot to remind their slaves who was in charge.

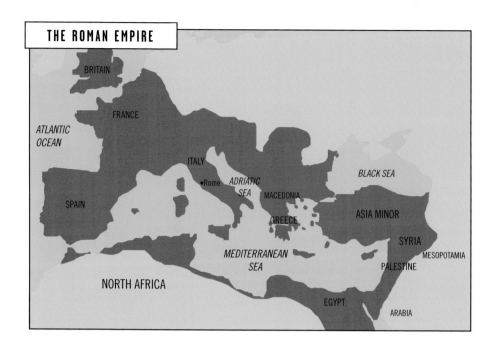

THE ROMAN EMPIRE

Buying Slaves

It was not hard to buy a slave, if you could afford one. Greek slaves were displayed for sale at the marketplace, the agora, along with meat, vegetables, cheese, and other food. Sellers had to announce sales in advance, so that people could object to the sale of a particular slave. They also had to guarantee that the slave had no defects such as a violent temper. If they lied, the slave could be returned for a refund.

Slave dealers traveled alongside the Roman armies, ready to buy up captives. Victorious military commanders decided for themselves which ones would be presented to the state, which would be given to the soldiers, which would be killed on the spot, and which would be sold.

The dealers chained together the captives who would be sold and set up temporary markets in order to sell them. Buyers examined the captives as if they were farm animals, peering at their bodies and feeling their muscles. Roman slave dealers had to list the slave's age and physical markings in deeds of sale. As in Greece, they had to warn buyers of any slave "defects" such as an extreme interest in religion, the arts, or love. These interests showed passion, and a passionate nature might make a slave hard to control. If the seller gave incorrect information, he would have to repay the buyer twice the price of the slave.

Whether the sale was in the Greek agora or in a makeshift market near a Roman battleground, men cost more than women or children, and skilled workers cost more than unskilled ones. Child slaves cost less because of the expense of raising them and the uncertainty of their future. Would they be tall or puny, weak or strong, healthy or sickly?

Kidnappers and pirates also took part in the slave trade. On land or sea they overpowered people and carried them off to the slave market. Wealthy families were sometimes fortunate enough to be able to buy back their loved ones. The desperate poor did as such people had always done; they sold themselves or their children into slavery to avoid starvation. Slave traders who found abandoned babies were allowed to claim them to sell as well.

Less Than a Person

There is no question that in the Bible slaves are considered human beings, but this was not so in Greece and Rome. Greeks called slaves *andrapoda*, which means "man-footed beings," and Romans called them little ones or little boys regardless of their age. Owners named their slaves as if they were pets, or kept the names the dealers had given them on the auction block, which often promised an admirable quality – perhaps Hilarus for "cheerful" or Celer for "swift." The degradation continued with the owners branding the slaves with hot irons, and speaking to them as if they were children.

To the owners, the very fact that people were slaves proved that they were inferior. It did not matter what the slave thought, felt, or had done before enslavement. Most people shared the opinion of the famous Greek philosopher Aristotle, who wrote, "A man who is able to belong to another person is by nature a slave (for that is why he belongs to someone else)."

A far less common point of view was heard in a comic play by the writer Philemon, who had a character say, "Though one is a slave, he is a man no less than you, master; he is made of the same flesh. No one is a slave by nature; it is fate that enslaves the body." Although some people questioned whether slavery was a natural condition, no one tried to end the practice.

JULIUS CAESAR, CAPTURED

Julius Caesar – the famous Roman statesman, conqueror, and emperor – was once captured by pirates. When he was a twenty-five-year-old praetor (similar to a magistrate), he was captured by pirates who plagued the Mediterranean Sea. These buccaneers sold most of their captives to Romans, but they demanded ransom from wealthy prisoners.

The pirates didn't know who Caesar was, but they could tell that he was rich, so they asked for twenty talents of silver to free him. Caesar laughed at them, offered fifty, and sent his men to raise the funds. For thirty-eight days, until they returned, he acted as if he were the pirates' keeper instead of their prisoner. He joined them in their games and exercises, and wrote poems and speeches that he read to them. If they did not praise his work, he insulted them and threatened to have them hanged.

After the ransom was paid, Caesar raised a fleet, captured the pirates, and had them imprisoned. He wanted them executed, but the governor wanted to sell them into slavery instead. Caesar returned to the prison, claimed the pirates for himself, and crucified them – as he had said he would when he was their captive.

Owners expected slaves to devote themselves to their work, submit to their masters' wishes, be loyal to them, and make them feel superior. Many slaves were so hungry for human attachments that they became the faithful servants their owners wanted. One man who had been enslaved by a Roman for forty years said:

> I did all I could to gratify my master, who was an honorable and worthy man. And in the house I was dealing with people who would have liked nothing better than to trip me up. But in the end I came out on top, praise be to my master! Now, that is real merit, because to be born free isn't very hard at all.

Most slaves found their situation more difficult. They had no control over where they worked or what their owners might do. Owners could punish them with branding, burning, flogging, tattooing, and maiming, for minor misdeeds or none at all.

Tools for Any Task

Some slaves did not have human owners; they were owned by the state. In Athens, for example, city slaves worked as inspectors of weights and measures, heralds, accountants, executioners, and scribes. But most slaves were seen as possessions of an individual. The average Greek home had three slaves and wealthy households had about fifty, including ten or twenty female slaves who did household chores like fetching water, sewing, tending children, and cleaning. Even a chore that sounds simple, such as serving food, could be humiliating; some serving women were forced to wear a device called a throat choke to prevent them from sneaking any of their master's food.

The Romans had far larger households, and because they frowned on all manual work, they needed far more slaves. A modest household might have just two or three slaves, but a moderately rich family might own four hundred or more. One Roman slave owner took eight hundred personal slaves and shepherds with him when he went to war. The general who fought Spartacus owned approximately twenty thousand slaves.

If they needed advice on how to choose and manage slaves, ancient slave owners could turn to instruction books. One writer suggested that they feed their slaves well to keep them from stealing, provide more food for harder work and less if slaves were too ill to work, sell slaves when they became old, and give them just a shirt, cloak, and wooden shoes every two years. Another writer recommended separating slaves from the same nation to prevent them from talking and possibly fighting.

Though many slaves were highly skilled, their owners usually got the credit for their work. A wealthy Greek politician, for example, used slaves in the Olympics in 416 BCE. He had seven chariots entered in one race, but he hadn't devoted years of his life to grueling preparation and training. Instead, slaves had built the chariots, groomed and trained the horses, and even helped build the stadium for the event. And it was the politician's slaves who risked their lives driving the chariots when the dangerous competition began. When the chariots proved victorious, however, the medals and prize money all went to their owner – not to the slaves.

Wealthy women depended on slaves to bathe them, clothe them, do their hair, and accompany them when they left their homes. This wall painting shows ladies of Pompeii, in today's Italy, with their slave hairdresser.

Sometimes the only job a slave had was to be a status symbol, like jewelry or fashionable clothes. Free men and women flaunted their wealth by taking slaves with them when they appeared in public, even if they were just making a social visit to a neighbor. The poet Horace did not even acknowledge his slave's presence when he wrote, "I am accustomed to walking alone," although a few lines later he made it clear that his slave was with him.

Most slaves were not status symbols but laborers doing exhausting, dangerous jobs. One of the worst places to work was in the mines. At the silver mine in Laurion, near Athens, Greece, as many as thirty thousand men and women, weak and strong, slaved in the mine pits and processing areas. The conditions were horrible. The historian Diodorus Siculus shows a sensitivity to their misery that is unusual for his time:

A pottery storage jar shows a Greek slave (seated on the right) holding a sandal. On the left, the shoemaker, who may also have been a slave, is cutting the leather around the woman customer's foot.

The workers in these mines produce incredible profits for the owners, but their own lives are spent underground in the quarries wearing and wasting their bodies day and night. Many die, their sufferings are so great. There is no relief, no respite from their labors. The hardships to which the overseer's lash compels them to submit are so severe that, except for a few, whose strength of body and bravery of soul enable them to endure for a long time, they abandon life, because death seems preferable. . . . No leniency or respite of any kind is given to any man who is sick, or maimed, or aged, or in the case of a woman for her weakness, but all without exception are compelled by blows to persevere in their labors, until through ill-treatment they die in the midst of their tortures.

Humans for Rent

In Greece and Rome, as in Mesopotamia centuries earlier, owners could rent out their slaves. Sometimes the work was harsh – miners were often owned by one person and rented by another. Other slaves had easier lives. In Greece, slaves who were hired out, particularly in cities, lived apart from their owners, often because the owners' houses didn't have room for them. These slaves were sometimes called paybringers because they brought income to their owners. We can still see the paybringers' beautiful handiwork in buildings, mosaics, leather goods, and vases that have survived. Paybringers were allowed to keep a little of the money they earned. A stone mason who worked with his slaves on the Acropolis in Athens was paid for his own work and given a share of his slaves' pay as well. Other paybringers were bankers, shop and factory managers, and captains of trading vessels.

The Rule of Law

Workers today expect to have rights under the law. The only rights the slaves had were those their owners felt like giving them, and owners could change their minds on a whim. If an owner broke a promise to a slave, the slave could do nothing about it. The law was overwhelmingly on the owner's side.

The leaders of Rome, known as the consuls, issued the Law of the Twelve Tables, which laid out the basic laws of the land. These included such penalties as the enslavement of people in debt, and a fine for breaking someone's bone. The fine for breaking a free person's bone was twice that for breaking a slave's bone. Some laws addressed the punishment of slaves who had committed crimes. Masters could punish slaves as they chose, but they did not want the punishment to reflect badly on their own reputation. A Roman poet wrote that a woman who scratched her hairdresser or stabbed her with a needle did not make herself attractive.

Spartacus's heroic escape has been celebrated in books and even in movies. Despite threats of branding and crucifixion, countless other slaves whose names we will never know also tried to run away. When they ran off, Roman owners advertised rewards for their capture, consulted oracles, astrologers, and dream interpreters, got help from public authorities, and even hired professional slave catchers. For those who escaped while serving in a war, freedom might depend on who won. Sometimes, the peace treaty said that fugitives and deserters would be handed back to the side they had abandoned.

The greatest punishment was reserved for a slave who killed a master. About two thousand years ago, a slave killed a senior Roman official. The law said that the official's other four hundred slaves must be killed. Freedmen – people who once had been enslaved but had been freed – protested the penalty, and the Roman senate debated the issue. Most senators voted in favor of death for all the slaves, and Emperor Nero ordered that the savage punishment be carried out.

A Path to Freedom

It is hard to imagine how slaves felt when they heard that somebody they knew had been freed. Owners had different reasons for freeing their slaves, but they often held out the possibility of freedom as a way to make slaves work hard. Manumission – the freeing of slaves – could only happen if the owners agreed. Some slaves managed to raise money to buy their freedom. They usually worked in places like stores or workshops, where they could try to save up tips, presents, or payments for the things they made. Greek slaves who had not saved enough could borrow from loan clubs formed by the slaves themselves. We know of slaves in Rome who invested in their masters' business and in time owned land, a house, or even a business of their own.

Roman masters even made financial provision for slaves before freeing them. In return, the ex-slaves were tied to their masters, who had become their patrons. Typically ex-slaves were expected to pay ceremonial calls on their patrons every day, and sometimes to pay them from their earnings. Some former slaves continued to serve their previous masters in almost the same way they had when they were slaves. In Rome ex-slaves were citizens. In Greece they were not; they were a class apart, neither slaves nor citizens.

On rare occasions, an extraordinary slave would be freed out of gratitude for his work. One of these, Pasion, became one of the richest men in Greece. He had served two bankers and had been so good at his work that he had been promoted to the position of chief clerk. Later, when he was freed, he continued to work for the bankers. Pasion was so successful that he gave the government money when it was needed. In turn, he was rewarded with citizenship. When he retired, he turned the bank's management over to his own slave, whom he then freed.

Owners sometimes granted freedom to a slave who was near death so that the person could die with dignity as a freed man. They might also bequeath freedom to their slaves in their wills, to show, when they themselves died, that they had been good masters.

Any children born to freed slaves would also be free, but children born while the parents were slaves would remain slaves unless they could buy their own freedom. And that, unfortunately, was rare. Most Greek and Roman slave owners never gave up control, and their slaves never became free.

CHAPTER 3
SAINTS AND VIKINGS: EUROPE IN THE MIDDLE AGES

Most slaves are buried in unmarked graves, their names forever lost to history. But one former slave is honored with festivities every year on St. Patrick's Day, March 17.

He was born Patricius in Britain around the year 390 CE, at a time when the land was part of the Roman Empire and its official language was Latin. Patricius – or Patrick – grew up surrounded by slaves on his wealthy parents' estate. Irish pirates raided his home when he was not yet sixteen years old, capturing him and carrying him off to Ireland. He went from being the privileged son in a comfortable home to being a slave tending sheep. Patrick spent day after tedious day on the lonely hills, cold, hungry, and with only the sheep for company. His family in Britain were Christian but had not been very religious. In Ireland, however, Patrick began to pray.

When he was twenty-one years old, Patrick escaped. He traveled about two hundred miles (300 km), until he came to a ship. Its captain first refused to give him passage back home but later relented. Back in Britain, Patrick dedicated himself to his faith, eventually becoming a bishop in the Church. In about 430, the Church returned him to Ireland. Patrick converted thousands to Christianity and fought against the enslavement of Christians with a passion drawn from his own experiences. (Though the Church did not oppose all slavery, it was against the enslavement of Christians by non-Christians.) He especially condemned the enslavement of women, who "suffer the most," he said, enduring "terrors and constant threats."

When the British king Coroticus invaded Ireland, he and his men slaughtered many newly baptized Christians and captured people of all ages. Patrick tried to ransom the slaves, but Coroticus merely laughed at his efforts. Patrick's hands were tied; he could neither fight Coroticus nor talk him into freeing his captives. He tried persuasion of a different type. Since many of Coroticus's soldiers were Christians, Patrick wrote a letter to be read aloud to the king and his men. "You . . . murder them and sell them to an outlandish race which does not know God," he wrote. He hoped the men would convince their king to free the captives. No documents exist to tell us whether he was successful.

This statue of Saint Patrick – the one-time slave shepherd – stands in Westport, County Mayo, Ireland. The lamb represents Christianity, and the snake on his staff refers to the belief that Saint Patrick drove all the snakes out of Ireland.

THE MEANING OF "SLAVE"

Originally, the words for "slave" in most European languages came from the word *servus*, which meant "slave" in Latin. But during the Middle Ages, those words were applied not to slaves but simply to people of the lowest classes. Meanwhile, the largest group of slaves purchased by Europeans came from the Slavic lands – the parts of Europe north and west of the Black Sea, including today's Russia, Ukraine, Belarus, Serbia, and Bulgaria. The ethnic name "Slav" was soon applied to all slaves: *slav* in English, *esclave* in French, *esclavo* in Spanish, *escravo* in Portuguese, *schiavo* in Italian, and *Sklave* in German. As for those words derived from *servus*, they came to mean the class of serfs, the peasants in the feudal system of the Middle Ages.

Today the Catholic Church reveres Saint Patrick as the apostle of Ireland, and people in many countries – Catholic and non-Catholic, Irish and non-Irish alike – wear green on St. Patrick's Day to honor this former slave.

Raiders from the North

For another thousand years or so after Patrick's death – in a period known as the Middle Ages – slavery continued in Europe, and being Christian was no guarantee of being spared. The threat of captivity persisted in Europe until the nineteenth century.

Some three hundred years after the Irish captured Patrick, other marauders – Vikings – stormed the coasts of Ireland and Britain. The Vikings came from Scandinavia (Norway, Sweden, and Denmark). Among them were expert boatmen, traders, adventurers, and settlers, but also bandits, kidnappers, and murderers who terrorized the people they encountered on shore.

The Viking era was launched in the spring of 793 with a murderous attack on Lindisfarne, a monastery perched high atop a small rocky island off the coast of northeastern England. When an English churchman heard about the ferocious raid, he wrote:

> . . . never before has such an atrocity been seen in Britain as we have now suffered at the hands of a pagan people. Such a voyage was not thought possible. The church of St. Cuthbert is spattered with the blood of the priests of God, stripped of all its furnishings, exposed to the plundering of the pagans.

The Vikings were after the church's gold and bejeweled treasures, including the beautifully decorated biblical text known as the Lindisfarne Gospels. Along with the loot they took captives to become slaves.

Even though they were Scandinavians themselves, the Vikings showed no mercy when it came to raiding Scandinavian villages and enslaving their own people. They rampaged right across Europe to Russia. They were not the only slave traders doing such terrible work: in Wales, traders sold their own countryfolk to the Vikings. There were probably others who turned against their own people for profit.

What was it like to be captured by Vikings? An eleventh-century German historian described a Viking raid in lands that now include parts of the Netherlands and Germany:

> At that time a fleet of the pirates whom our people call Ascomanni landed in Saxony and devastated all the coastland of Frisia and Hadeln. And, as they went up the mouth of the Elbe River, they fell upon the province. . . . The victorious Swedes and Danes completely destroyed the whole Saxon troop. Captured there were the margrave [governor] Siegfried, Count Dietrich and other distinguished men whom the barbarians dragged to the ships with their hands tied behind their backs, and their feet shackled with chains. After that the barbarians ravaged the whole province with impunity.

The Vikings sometimes freed captives – for a price. The abbey of St-Denis, in France, spent an immense sum as ransom for its abbot – more than the Church had paid the Vikings earlier that year to keep them from burning the city of Paris.

The Image of Slaves

People through the ages have justified taking slaves by telling themselves that they were not quite human. The Vikings described their slaves in such ugly terms that it seemed to give them an excuse for treating them terribly.

Scandinavian slaves were known as thralls, and wherever they lived, and wherever they had come from, they were forever outsiders. The thralls left no record of how they felt about their lives, but the sagas and eddas, the epic poems of the time, have survived, and they give us a vivid picture of how free people felt about thralls.

In the poem "The Lay of Rig," the god Rig visits three households and has a son with the woman in each one. His eldest son, Träl ("Slave"), and his family are described cruelly:

> A swarthy boy was born to Edda.
> She sprinkled water on him, called him Träl
> Black were his nails, his face was ugly
> Gnarled were his joints, crooked his back,
> Thick were his fingers, and his feet were long.

AN EARLY EFFORT AT FREEDOM

Slavery was accepted under Catholic Church law in the Middle Ages, but the law frowned on sending Christians as slaves to serve pagans. Around 850 in northeast Germany, a band of pagans captured Christians and held them as slaves. Some of the captives fled to neighboring Christians for refuge. Rather than help them, the neighbors bound them in chains, sold some to pagans and others to Christians, and enslaved the rest themselves.

The Archbishop Anskar (or Ansgar) objected to keeping Christians enslaved. He traveled to the noblemen in charge to get these captives freed, and to ensure that they would not be captured again. Today, the archbishop is known as Saint Anskar, the Apostle of the North.

Träl grows up and meets a girl with dirty feet and a "down-bent nose." They have twenty-one children, all with insulting names like Brat, Clod, and Sluggard for their sons, and Clumsy-girl and Servant-girl for their daughters. This repulsive family were supposed to be the ancestors of all the thralls.

Of course, the slaves in Scandinavia didn't look much different from free people, especially those slaves who were Scandinavian themselves. And even if some did look different, it is heartbreaking to think that they were supposed to be less than human because of their appearance. But the poem shows a view of slaves as ugly, dirty, and cowardly, and of free people as handsome, brave, and noble.

Not all sagas showed slaves in such a hateful light. Some show that free people valued their loyal slaves. In one saga the thrall Asgaut is described as a large man with a shapely body, "And though he was called a thrall, yet few could be found his equal amongst those called freemen, and he knew well how to serve his master." That was high, rare praise for a slave.

Slavery Laws in the Viking Homelands

Scandinavia included many kingdoms, each with its own laws about slavery. In Denmark, masters were responsible for the crimes of their slaves; if the master denied that the slave had committed the crime, the slave could be tortured with a hot iron to make him confess. An Icelandic law required the owner of a slave suspected of theft to swear an oath on the slave's behalf – otherwise the slave could be flogged, mutilated, or beheaded. But sometimes the law was more forgiving toward a slave. If a slave committed a crime at the owner's request, the slave would often go free. Someone who insulted, injured, or killed a free man had to pay the injured person or his family money for damaging his honor. Someone other than a slave's owner who injured or killed the slave had to pay the owner. The payment was for harm to the owner's property; honor had nothing to do with it.

In Norway, masters could treat their own slaves however they wanted, including killing them. The only law against killing a slave was one that warned such murderers that they'd have to answer to God.

Freedom

In Scandinavia, as in Ancient Greece and Rome, an owner might free a slave in gratitude, or a slave might be freed after the owner died. Slaves could also buy their freedom with any money they were permitted to earn. But even after they'd been freed, former slaves didn't have all the rights of a freeborn person. They might not be allowed to marry, to have their own households, or to conduct a business. They couldn't even choose who would inherit their possessions after their death; their former owners would be their heirs.

Burials

Slaves could be sacrificed at their owner's death in order to serve him in the next life. The Arab traveler Ahmad ibn Fadlan witnessed a ship burial and human sacrifice in the year 921. He reported that the family turned to the slaves after the chieftain's death and asked, "Who among you will die with him?"

> One of them said, "I shall." So they placed two slave-girls in charge of her to take care of her and accompany her wherever she went, even to the point of occasionally washing her feet with their own hands. They set about attending to the dead man, preparing his clothes for him and setting right all he needed. Every day the slave-girl would drink alcohol and would sing merrily and cheerfully.

The people prepared the chieftain for burial and readied the ship where they would place him and the slave girl, supplying it with food, alcohol, fruit, herbs, weapons, and other things they thought the dead man would need. They also prepared the slave girl for her death. An interpreter explained the ritual to Ibn Fadlan:

> The first time they lifted her, she said, "Behold, I see my father and my mother." The second time she said, "Behold, I see all of my dead kindred, seated." The third time she said, "Behold, I see my master, seated in Paradise. Paradise is beautiful and verdant [green]. He is accompanied by his men and his male slaves. He summons me, so bring me to him." So they brought her to the ship and she removed two bracelets that she was wearing, handing them to the woman called the "Angel of Death," the one who was to kill her.

The woman stabbed the slave and placed her beside her dead master. A relative of the chieftain set fire to the ship, which was then pulled from the fire and buried.

The name of the chieftain and the name of the king were written on a piece of birch as a grave marker. They did not name the girl.

The End of Viking Slavery

The Vikings' early successes had depended on surprise. After years of attacks, towns and villages could no longer be taken so easily. They were prepared to fight off the Vikings with strong forces of their own. Raiding also became less common among the Vikings themselves.

Although people continued to keep slaves in the Viking homelands for the next few hundred years, the practice gradually faded away, there and elsewhere in Northern Europe. No one knows exactly when it ended, or why. Experts think the spread of Christianity had an influence, in part because the Church encouraged owners to treat slaves well and free individual slaves. Indeed, a Swedish law in 1335 prohibited the enslavement of anyone who had a Christian mother or father.

A Booming Slave Trade

Meanwhile, slavery continued in other lands. In northern Italy, for example, slaves became part of almost every household. They had not been an important part of life there for two hundred years, but a terrible disease was about to change everything.

The Black Death – the dreaded plague – swept through Europe and North Africa, Syria, and Iraq from 1348 to 1350. For those who witnessed the spread of the disease, it must have seemed like the end of the world. Some victims suffered from big dark boils, high fevers, and diarrhea before they died in agony. Others dropped dead before they even knew they were sick. There were carts full of corpses, but there was nowhere left to dump them. Whole villages disappeared, with nobody left to bury the last person alive. No one knows exactly how many people died, but it was probably about seventy-five million – more than one-third of the Western world's population.

In the Italian town of Florence alone, half the people died. The plague infected both rich and poor, but the poor were hit harder because they lived in more crowded conditions. The rich were desperate to replace the servants who had perished, but the workers who had survived had their pick of jobs – and not many

This illustration, from a French book handwritten around 1350, suggests the misery and desperation caused by the plague. As people fled infected towns, they carried the disease and spread it.

wanted to be servants. The leaders of Florence had a solution: they would revive slavery. In 1363, they ruled that Florentines could import foreign slaves as long as they were not Christians.

Import them they did. Most prized were young slaves, especially girls. The children were as young as eight, and most were under eighteen.

Young Slaves

"Pray buy for me a little slave-girl, young and sturdy and of good stock, strong and able to work hard . . . so that I can bring her up in my own way, and she will learn better and quicker and I shall get better service out of her," the wealthy business-man Francesco Datini wrote in 1393. "I want her only to wash the dishes and carry the wood and bread to the oven, and work of that sort . . . for I have another one here who is a good slave and can cook and serve well."

The children included Greeks, Russians, Turks, Slavs, Cretans, Arabs, and Ethiopians. They were packed on ships as if they were bales of cloth or vats of

THE CRUSADE INTO SLAVERY

Nicholas was a German boy, perhaps no more than twelve, in the year 1212, when he led thousands of people, mostly children, on a crusade from Germany to Jerusalem. That same year, a twelve-year-old French boy, Stephen, inspired thousands of children to join him in going "to God." Together these expeditions are known as the Children's Crusade.

Tens of thousands of older Christians had already marched in four crusades from Western Europe, across mountains and deserts, in unsuccessful attempts to reclaim the Holy Land from the Muslims. The children wanted to succeed where their elders had failed. The German crusade began, one chronicler wrote, when "many thousands of boys, ranging in age from six years to full maturity, left the plows or carts which they were driving, the flocks which they were pasturing, and anything else which they were doing." Their parents urged them to turn back, but many walked over the snow-covered Alps into Italy, finding hunger, thirst, exhaustion, and disap-pointment along the way.

Some of the children remained in Genoa, in Italy, but others walked on to other port cities, still hoping to get to the Holy Land. Instead, they met with tragedy. Pirates lured them to their ships and sold them as slaves. Of all the children who left Germany, only a handful ever returned home.

Most historians say the children following Stephen through France became hungry and tired, and the king commanded them to go home. But one account tells a different story. A clergyman who arrived in France from Egypt in 1230 said he had been one of Stephen's followers. He said the children had numbered thirty thousand when they arrived in Marseilles. There, two men had offered seven ships to take them across the Mediterranean Sea. Two of the vessels had been shipwrecked, drowning everyone on board. The others had landed on the North African coast. The men had sold some of the children into slavery there, and had taken the others to Baghdad, where they too were sold. He said that he had eventually escaped, but the other children — now grown up — were still in slavery.

olive oil. One vessel that left Romania in 1396 listed "17 bales of pilgrims' robes, 191 pieces of lead, and 80 slaves."

The voyage from their native land must have been terrifying. Captured children would be taken to a large slave market in Genoa, Venice, or Pisa, where a dealer would buy them. Their hands or faces would be marked with cuts or tattoos to identify them as slaves. Imagine the pain, seasickness, terror, and fear of what might happen next.

Slaves of all religions were bought and sold, but soon after they arrived they would be taken to a church where a priest would baptize them as Christians and give them new names. Some owners worried about this baptism. By law they could not import Christian slaves; would they have to free the slaves once they were baptized? Religious leaders assured them that they would not. One of them explained that the baptism of slaves was meaningless, and "to baptize such men is like baptizing oxen."

The seller would draw up a deed of sale that stated each slave's place of birth and described his or her appearance. The descriptions were not kind. In a list of 357 slaves registered in Florence, only one was described as handsome. Most descriptions were like the one that said a seventeen-year-old girl had "a wideish face, snub and thick nose, many moles in her face." As they had centuries before, sellers were supposed to guarantee their slaves' health and good morals.

The days ahead would be hard for the young slaves. There were so many restrictions — even on what they wore. Free girls and women could adorn themselves with bright colors and soft fabrics, but the laws required slave women to wear clothing of coarse gray wool, or black capes with natural-colored dresses — no purples or reds for them, no silk gowns, no belts with golden threads. On their heads they could wear only a linen towel with a black stripe, and on their feet only wooden clogs with black straps.

The chores that Datini described — "wash the dishes and carry the wood and bread to the oven, and work of that sort" — were not as easy as he made them sound. Household labor was tedious and full of risk. The dishwater was scalding, the wood was heavy, and the bread oven was dangerously hot.

Owners' Rights

In the formal writing of a contract, sellers typically gave owners permission to "have, hold, sell, alienate, exchange, enjoy, rent or unrent, to dispose of in his will, to judge soul and body" and generally to do whatever they pleased with their slaves.

Owners must have known that their slaves were often miserable, resentful, and angry, because they certainly didn't trust them. Margherita Datini, Francesco's wife, called them female beasts and said, "You cannot trust the house to them: they might at any moment rise up against you."

Owners were especially afraid that their slaves would put magic potions or poisons in their food, and the law called for drastic punishment of slaves suspected of such treachery. A female slave in Venice who poisoned her mistress was branded, whipped, and had her nose and lips cut off. A male slave in the same town had his eyes put out for poisoning his master's food.

Escape must have been on every slave's mind, but it was almost impossibly hard. How to hide the scars? How to get a change of clothes? It was illegal to try to escape, and slaves who were caught were considered thieves for stealing their owner's property – themselves.

Even if they got away, where would they go? Everyone would be on the look-out for a runaway, and anyone found helping one would face a heavy fine or punishment. The town officials would issue a proclamation like this one:

> . . . whoever shall hold or keep or know who is holding or keeping a certain slave belonging to Piero di Dato, called Bernardina, 16 years old, with a brown gown and a black overcoat and shall not give her back to the said Piero, or give information to the Office of the said Eight [the City police] within three days from the date of this proclamation shall be arrested and considered guilty of theft and proceeded against according to the Law.

Slaves were almost always caught and sent back, since their clothes, cuts or tattoos, and mannerisms made it clear that they were fugitives. But there was an exception: a slave who was Christian and belonged to a Jew could take refuge in a church, where he or she would be safe.

There was only one realistic route to freedom: receiving it as a gift from the owner. People often freed their slaves in their wills, because they believed the act would atone for their sins. Francesco Datini's will said that he freed "for the love of God, every slave of mine in any and every part of the world, restoring to them their pristine liberty."

This portrait, drawn by the famous artist Albrecht Dürer in 1521, shows a mixed-race woman who was the slave of a Portuguese man. All we know of her is her name, Catherine.

ALMOST A SLAVE

Nikolai Shipov was not a slave, but you could easily mistake him for one. He had an owner who could whip him whenever he chose, or even sell him. But his owner also let him travel to conduct business, just as Nikolai's father had done. Nikolai was a serf.

Slavery had existed in Russia for centuries, but it had ended by the time Nikolai Shipov was born, in 1802. Serfdom had taken its place. Starting in the tenth century, serfs had gradually replaced slaves in France, England, Germany, Poland, and elsewhere in Europe. The laws regulating serfs varied with each country and changed over the centuries, but they were generally peasants who had to pay the landowner, usually a nobleman, for the right to work the land. In many places, landowners could not sell serfs away from the land, nor could they sell the land away from the serfs. The two were bound to each other.

Nikolai and his father were livestock traders with a sideline in furs, leather, and tallow (animal fat). Successful as they were, they never got the rewards they wanted because of the demands of their owner, Saltykov, and his manager, Raguzin. Every year, Nikolai's father had to pay Saltykov five thousand rubles. In 1830, he told Raguzin that he would pay fifty

One unfortunate slave was supposed to be freed, but her owner died before he could complete the arrangement. A document he left said clearly that he wanted to free his Russian slave Margherita "in view of the love, solicitude and fidelity" with which she had served him. For nine years after his death, however, his mother made Margherita work as a slave, even renting her to another family for four years. Finally she freed Margherita, saying she was "moved by charity."

Those who were freed still faced obstacles. With no money or skills, they often had no choice but to beg or steal.

The use of slavery in Italy began to decline around six hundred years ago. Wars blocked the trade routes for Italian slave ships, so slaves were harder to import. This didn't stop the very rich from getting slaves from Greece and the Slavic lands, and from Africa, but these slaves often served more as decoration than as workers. A high Church official, Cardinal Ippolito de' Medici, used enslaved Arabs and Turks as horsemen, Africans as wrestlers, and Indians as divers, and when he died, his slaves carried his corpse from his country house to Rome. Still, they were slaves, far from home. The very rich remained slave owners until the 1800s.

J.B. le Prince del.   J.B. Tilliard Sculp.

SUPPLICE DU GRAND KNOUT.

thousand if Saltykov freed his son. When Raguzin refused, Nikolai ran away, but he returned within months when he heard that his father was ill.

His father died a short time later. Nikolai appealed to Raguzin again for his freedom, and again the manager refused.

Nikolai's chance came when he discovered a law that said that serfs who were "captured by mountain plunderers would be freed along with all their family upon escaping from captivity." To make this work, Nikolai had to escape, get himself captured, and then flee his captors. He fled to the Caucasus Mountains, where he was soon caught. His plan succeeded. Eight months after his capture and fifteen years after his father's offer to buy his freedom, Nikolai and his family became free.

Russians used a whip called a knout to punish slaves and serfs. It had a long handle attached to a strip of treated leather, as hard as metal. The leather was replaced after about ten lashes, to be sure it was stiff enough to inflict terrible pain. Victims did not always survive a beating.

CHAPTER 4
IN THE REALM OF THE QUR'AN: SLAVERY UNDER ISLAM

For centuries, black-skinned people, originally from East Africa and known as the Zanj, had been forced into slavery in Iraq. Under a blazing sun they did the backbreaking work of removing layers of salt from marshland, digging ditches, and planting sugar and cotton, all the while living in squalid camps of five hundred to five thousand workers.

The slaves first revolted in the year 694, but that uprising was easily put down. Two hundred years passed before a dynamic leader came forward to lead the downtrodden slaves to revolt again. That leader was Ali ibn Muhammad.

In 869, Ali ibn Muhammad arrived in the city of Basra. He was not a slave himself, but he promised to give slaves a better life – land, money, even slaves of their own. He attracted an army of fifteen thousand Zanj slaves, peasants, and poor city-dwellers.

Was Ali ibn Muhammad a visionary, or power-hungry? One historian who wrote about the Zanj revolt shortly after it took place called him "an abominable one," an enemy of Allah (God). Another chronicler reported that the Zanj massacred "children and old people, men and women, and everywhere sowed fire and destruction."

But Ali ibn Muhammad was also admired as a man who showed mercy to his enemies. He gathered slave owners together and told them, "I wanted to behead you all for the way you have treated these slaves, with arrogance and coercion and, indeed, in ways that Allah has forbidden, driving them beyond endurance. But my companions have spoken to me about you, and now I have decided to set you free."

When the masters warned him that the slaves would desert him, and offered to pay him to return them, he refused. He reassured the slaves, "Some of your number should watch me closely, and if they sense any treachery on my part, they could kill me." He remained loyal to the Zanj.

Eventually, however, many of his Zanj and Arab followers turned against him. Some say that he began to act a lot like the masters they were rebelling against, keeping booty for himself and his friends, and taxing his followers heavily.

In 883, the forces of the Islamic spiritual leader, the caliph, put down the Zanj's rebellion and Ali ibn Muhammad died in battle.

The Zanj Revolt may have influenced landowners in the Islamic world to shy away from using large numbers of slaves — gang slavery — for fear that slaves would band together and rebel. Their farms remained relatively small, and gang slavery was not the custom. But this does not mean that slavery disappeared. It was widespread in the Muslim world into the nineteenth century, and in some places it persists today.

The three great world religions based on a belief in one deity are Judaism, Christianity, and Islam, and slavery has been practiced by Jews, Christians, and Muslims alike. The Hebrew Bible never bans slavery, though the book of Exodus views the enslavement of the Hebrews in Egypt as a tragedy. The Christian Bible accepts slaves as a normal part of a community, although Paul, the founder of the Church, taught that all Christian believers were equal, saying, "there is neither bond nor free." The Prophet Muhammad founded the Islamic faith in Arabia in the first quarter of the seventh century. Within a hundred years, Islam had spread through Syria, Iraq, and Persia, as far east as the Indus Valley in India, and through North Africa and Spain in the west. Like Judaism and Christianity, Islam accepted slavery as part of everyday life.

Slavery and Islamic Law

Although Muhammad owned slaves himself and didn't forbid the practice, he taught that slaves and free people were equal in the eyes of God. He believed that slaves weren't just property; they had some rights, and their owners must treat them like fellow human beings:

A master should not act as though he despises or looks down on his slave.
A master should share his food with his slave and dress him as he dresses himself.
He should not overwork his slave or punish him harshly.
He should forgive his slave if the slave has done wrong.

These dark-skinned Zanj slaves staging a revolt against the Arabs in Iraq seem to be as well armed as their masters. This sixteenth-century manuscript is from India.

BARBARY CAPTIVITY

Americans and Europeans who traveled by ship in the seventeenth and eighteenth centuries risked capture by "Barbary pirates" who worked for North African regimes, including Morocco, Algiers, and Tripoli. If their governments did not pay a ransom, they might never return.

On October 25, 1793, the American brig *Polly*, two days away from her destination on the Spanish coast, encountered a ship flying an English flag. A sailor, dressed like an Englishman, hailed the *Polly*, and the *Polly*'s captain identified his ship. At that point alarmed Americans saw other sailors dressed in Algerian clothes. As crewman John Foss explains in an account he wrote five years after his adventure:

> About one hundred of the Pirates, jumped on board, all armed; some, with Scimitars and Pistols, others with pikes, spears, lances, knives, &c. . . . As soon as they came on board our vessel, they made signs for us all to go forward, assuring us in several languages that if we did not obey their commands, they would immediately massacre us all.

After looting the ship of bedding, books, charts, and navigation tools, they stripped the clothes off the crew, leaving them in

If he and his slave don't get along, he should sell his slave to another master. He should treat his female slaves well and not separate a slave mother from her young child.

Muhammad urged slave owners to free their slaves, saying, "The man who frees a Muslim slave, God will free from hell, limb for limb." And if a slave asked to be free, the master was to allow the slave to buy his freedom; "if you know some good in them . . . give them of the wealth of God that He has given you." Freed slaves were supposed to respect their former masters, and their former masters had to ensure that the ex-slaves and their families did not live in poverty.

Under the laws of Islam, not everyone could be enslaved. A slave was either someone born to slave parents or someone captured in a holy war — a jihad, a war whose purpose was to spread the religion of Islam. A Muslim was not supposed to enslave another Muslim, nor were Muslims supposed to enslave *dhimmis* — that is, Jews and Christians, as well as Zoroastrians (members of an ancient Eastern faith). People of these faiths were supposed to be protected from slavery because they believed in one God, like Muslims. However, the laws were not always obeyed.

The Route to Slavery

Muslims' slaves came from many places and were captured in many ways. White slaves came from northern Spain, Central and Eastern Europe, and Asia, and black slaves came from Africa. Some had been captured in pirate raids at sea, some in jihads. Yet others were bought from raiders or traders.

All travel was dangerous, but it would be hard to imagine anything worse than the plight of slaves from Africa who were forced to cross the vast desert of the Sahara on foot. From the earliest times, only nomadic desert tribes had the skill to find their way across the shifting sands, and the camels to carry them. What relief these miserable travelers must have felt when they reached a rare oasis and could drink fresh water!

The desert route was harsh, but transport by sea was not much better. Some slaves were brought by boat across the Mediterranean Sea and along the coast to the Middle East; others were shipped from East Africa across the Red Sea, the Persian Gulf, or the Indian Ocean to be sold in Arabia, Iraq, Persia, Turkey or India.

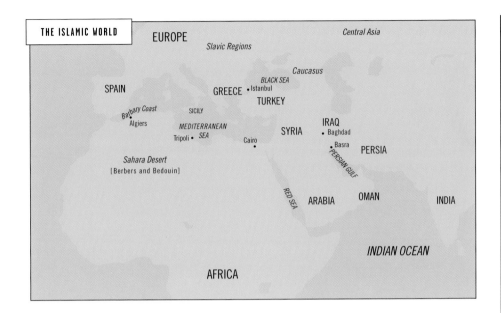

THE ISLAMIC WORLD

EUROPE

Central Asia

Slavic Regions

Caucasus

BLACK SEA

SPAIN

GREECE • Istanbul

TURKEY

Barbary Coast

SICILY

Algiers

MEDITERRANEAN
SEA

IRAQ
• Baghdad

SYRIA

Tripoli •

Cairo
•

• Basra

PERSIA

PERSIAN GULF

Sahara Desert
[Berbers and Bedouin]

RED SEA

ARABIA

OMAN

INDIA

INDIAN OCEAN

AFRICA

Conditions on Arab traders' ships were terrible, and slaves arrived in poor condition. Many died along the way.

The pirates who ravaged the Mediterranean coast were far from being swashbuckling characters in bright clothing and hoop earrings. They were cruel and dangerous thugs who preyed on innocent travelers. In the Middle Ages, Muslim raiders from Spain, Sicily, and North Africa carried off people from the Christian kingdoms along the Mediterranean. In turn, Christian pirates raided Muslim coastal areas. Like their enemies, they took prisoners and held them in slavery or for ransom.

Islam and Race

In the Muslim holy book, the Qur'an, the Prophet Muhammad teaches that God intentionally created people of many languages and colors, and says, "Among God's signs are the creation of the heavens and of the earth and the diversity of your languages and of your colors." Allah judges people not by their ethnic group or tribe but by their righteousness, he says. In fact, when Islam was a young religion, some of Muhammad's followers – including Umar, the second caliph – were of Ethiopian descent, and dark-skinned.

In his last sermon, Muhammad said, "No Arab has any priority over a non-Arab and no white over a black except in righteousness." But why did he find it

their underwear. They then ferried them to their own ship, whose captain made it clear that the captives would "experience the most abject slavery, on . . . arrival at Algiers, which we soon found to be true." They were presented to the governor of Algiers, who announced, "Now I have got you, you Christian dogs, you shall eat stones."

For the next three years, Foss and his companions endured wretched conditions in the Algerian prison where hundreds of Western captives were kept. Surviving on less than a pound (half a kilo) a day of grainy, sour bread and vinegar to dip it in, they spent long days blasting rocks and hauling them two miles (3 km) to build a breakwater in the harbor. To keep them working, the slave drivers were "continually beating the slaves with their sticks and goading them," says Foss. For minor misdeeds, men were bastinadoed – beaten with a stick hundreds of times on the back and the soles of the feet. Foss saw men tortured to death.

Almost two years after their capture, the American government bought freedom for the captives – too late for many who had already died of plague and other causes.

A NOTORIOUS SLAVE TRADER

South of the Sahara, the slave traders were not necessarily outsiders. Tippu Tip, named after the sound of his firearms, was an African-Arab trader from Zanzibar. His real name was Hamed bin Muhammad el Murjebi, and he established his own kingdom west of Lake Tanganyika in the 1860s. When a Christian missionary spotted one of Tip's caravans, the slaves had already come 1,000 miles (1,600 km) on foot from the Upper Congo, and had 250 more miles to go to reach the coast. Filthy, and scarred by the traders' whips, the captives were chained by the neck. Many of them were women with babies on their backs.

necessary to say this? It seems likely that he had begun to notice signs of racial or ethnic prejudice. We can find such signs in Arabic poetry, even as early as 660. For example, an African slave poet wrote, "If my color were pink, women would love me / But the Lord has marred me with blackness."

Tragically, when people have different skin color, features, and hair than the majority, they are often treated differently. And when they are the only people who do jobs nobody likes, such as cleaning streets or carrying garbage, it's a short step to believing that they are inferior.

At first, most slaves in the Middle East and the Mediterranean were white (from Spain, Greece, Eastern Europe, the Caucasus, and Central Asia), but as black slaves were imported into Islamic lands from more southerly parts of Africa, chilling comments started to appear in Arabic literature. "Is there anything more vile than black slaves, of less good and more evil than they?" wrote one medieval Egyptian poet.

After a grueling march across the Sahara desert, or a wretched voyage in a crowded ship, slaves were sold in markets like this one in Cairo in the 1840s.

From the sixteenth through eighteenth centuries, thousands of captives from Europe, and later from America, spent long years at harsh labor in North Africa. Accounts written by ransomed captives were popular reading. In this 1859 engraving, a Western artist imagines the despair of the captives in an exotic desert setting complete with camels.

Race didn't hold everyone back. A successful ruler of Egypt in the tenth century was a black man, and in Muslim India in the fourteenth century some Ethiopian slaves became rulers. But in slave markets, white slaves fetched a higher price than darker-skinned ones.

Slaves' Jobs

In the vast Islamic world, most slaves worked in cities or villages rather than on the land. As happened in Rome centuries earlier, the more work slaves did, the less their owners were willing to do, until the owners came to believe that working with their hands was beneath them. Almost all cleaning, cooking, laundry, child care, and sewing was done by female slaves. Most gardeners, grooms for the horses, watchmen, or – if they appeared capable and trustworthy – clerks or agents in the master's business affairs were male slaves.

Entertainers

If you were a slave and had a gift for music, poetry, dance, or art, you might be sent to school in Baghdad, Córdoba (in Spain), or Medina (in Arabia). If you were

A missionary took this photograph of a young slave in Zanzibar around 1890. His master chained the boy to a thirty-two-pound (14.5-kg) timber as a punishment. The only way the child could move was by carrying the timber on his head.

a female slave and were a talented musician, you might find yourself in a chamber orchestra. In fact, in the Middle Ages most singers, dancers, and musicians in Muslim lands had originally been slaves. Ziryab, an Iraqi-born black singer, musician, and poet – his name means "blackbird" – was a freed Persian slave who started his career in the court in Baghdad. When he eventually moved to Spain, this amazing man introduced the Spanish to the five-string lute, as well as asparagus, sugar cane, cotton, and toothpaste and deodorant!

Harems and Eunuchs

Probably the largest single category of slaves in the Islamic world was made up of women in harems. A man was allowed to have four wives if he could treat them all equally. He was also permitted to keep other women as concubines to give him pleasure. Rich rulers sometimes had harems of thousands of women, while tradesmen might have one or two. White-skinned women were preferred, but when white slaves became rare and expensive in the nineteenth century, Africans were recruited.

Harems were guarded by eunuchs – men who had been castrated, just as we "fix" dogs and cats, so they were not capable of sexual acts. Eunuchs were considered more reliable in general, so they often had very responsible jobs in the palace, as assistants to the ruler.

Doing the Heavy Work

For centuries the memory of the Zanj Revolt may have made landowners wary of slave gangs, but where there were farms or plantations, the owners wanted slaves – a great many slaves – for the backbreaking work. Black slaves worked the date plantations of northeastern Arabia, and cultivated dates, grain, and vegetables in the oases of the Sahara. They toiled on Moroccan plantations. They did the perilous work of mining gold in Egyptian Nubia and salt in the Western Sahara, where it is said that no slave survived for more than five years. Over the course of about a hundred years, right into the nineteenth century, Arabs from Oman, on the northern and eastern coasts of the Arabian Peninsula, imported a total of 769,000 black slaves to work on immense grain, sugar, and clove plantations in East Africa and on the island of Zanzibar.

Soldiers

Over the last thousand years, Muslims have had whole armies made up of slaves. As Islam spread, the caliphs bought or captured boys and young men – Turks, Slavs, Berbers, and Africans – from bordering non-Islamic regions. Christian boys, for example, were bought, converted to Islam, and educated in military arts to become soldiers and officers.

One of the most remarkable groups of slave soldiers was the Turkish Mamluks of Egypt. In 1260, their forces stopped the westward march of the Mongol invaders from Central Asia, who had already swept through Iran and sacked the city of Baghdad. The Mamluks became the ruling class of Egypt and Syria and remained in power for 250 years.

Slavery in the Ottoman Empire

Slaves in Islamic lands did not leave behind diaries or other accounts of what they thought or felt, but by the nineteenth century, court records can tell us much about what happened to them. This was a time of huge change in the Islamic Ottoman Empire, centered in Turkey. Western ideas and technology, such as the telegraph and railroads, were influencing Ottoman society, and Britain had the greatest impact. The British had abolished slavery in their own empire by 1838 and had begun to campaign against it elsewhere.

Slavery was still legal in the Ottoman Empire. In fact, around five out of every hundred people were slaves. But slaves could go to court if they believed they were ill-treated, and the Ottoman courts were becoming more willing to listen to their complaints. Slaves even knew which British consuls or British ships would shelter runaways, and which judges would be more sympathetic to their stories of abuse.

Accounts like these show the winds of change blowing through the Ottoman Empire:

An enslaved African woman ran away to the British consul in Turkey, saying she'd been beaten and abused. The consul appealed to the Ottoman authority, the vizier, who recommended that the government buy the woman from her slaveholder and free her.

In another case, an enslaved African family appeared at the British consulate in Tripoli. Their owner had tried to sell the mother and child onto a boat that would

COTTON FOR THE WORLD

During the American Civil War (1860 – 1865), not enough cotton was being harvested in the United States, so there was a worldwide boom in Egyptian cotton. The family of Egypt's ruler, Muhammad Ali, put hundreds of slaves to work on its cotton plantation. Egyptian peasants, enriched by rising cotton prices, bought African slaves from Sudan so they could work more of their land and produce more cotton.

In the 1800s, the mighty British navy policed the world's oceans to suppress the international slave trade. This print from 1884 shows Africans freed from a slave trader's ship by HMS *Undine*. In the background are two British sailors.

take them to far-away Istanbul. The father had been locked up by his owner but had managed to escape to the docks and free his wife and child just before they boarded the vessel. The British vice-consul appealed to the governor general of the province, who not only freed the family but put the slaveholder in jail.

Still, no abolition movement ever took hold among the Ottoman Turks. Even educated people who favored reforms made excuses for their type of slavery; they said it was gentle, and overlooked the high death rate in caravans and on slave ships. Soon the British government began to pressure the Ottomans to put an end to the trade of thousands of African women through Egypt. When the Turks agreed to do this, religious leaders in Arabia were furious; banning the slave trade was actually against Islamic law, they said. They stirred up riots against the Turks, until the Ottoman government backed down and allowed the slave trade to continue.

Modern Islamic Slavery

In the late nineteenth century, when the British occupied Egypt and eventually controlled Sudan, the source of so many African slaves, they were able to suppress the slave trade. By the end of the century, enslavement of white people had disappeared and black slavery had been considerably reduced. But slavery still existed, as we know from travelers' accounts from all over the Middle East. A Danish Muslim visitor to Libya in 1930 reported on a slave market held every Thursday in Kufra.

In fact, in much of the Middle East slavery was not made illegal until between World War I and World War II – roughly 1918 to 1939. In Saudi Arabia it was not banned until 1962, and even today foreign workers are held there in slavelike conditions.

The last Islamic country to end slavery officially was Mauritania, which passed various ineffective laws curtailing the practice in 1901, 1905, 1961, and 1981. The most recent law, in 2007, abolished slavery, but no one has been prosecuted for continuing to have slaves. During the long civil war between North and South Sudan (1983-2005), armed militias kidnapped people and forced them to work on farms or in military camps. This type of slave raiding continues in the war-torn Darfur region, and slaves are still forced to work in the country's north.

THE NUMBERS

By the 1840s, Zanzibar was exporting between 13,000 and 15,000 slaves a year, from as far west as the Upper Congo, across the Arabian Sea to the Middle East and Persia. The total number deported over the centuries from Islamic regions is not easy to calculate. One scholar has estimated that about 11,500,000 black slaves were exported across the Sahara, across the Red Sea, and along the East African coast from the year 650 until 1900. This is close to the number traded across the Atlantic Ocean (about 12,000,000), but the Atlantic trade happened over a much shorter time, from the sixteenth through the nineteenth centuries.

CHAPTER 5
CARAVANS, CANOES, AND CAPTIVES: AFRICA

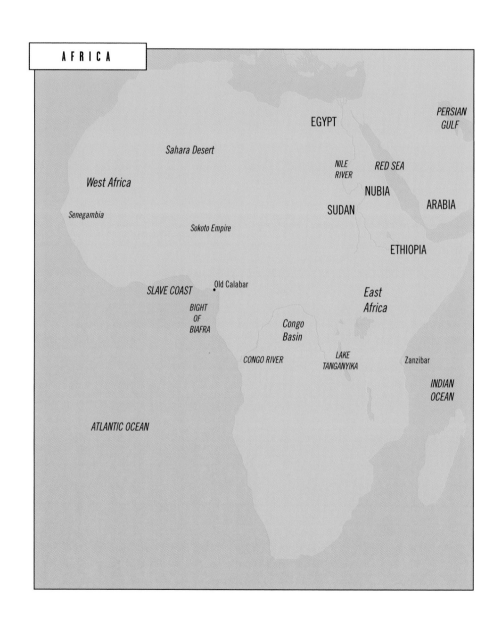

AFRICA

PERSIAN GULF

EGYPT

Sahara Desert

NILE RIVER

RED SEA

West Africa

NUBIA

Senegambia

SUDAN

ARABIA

Sokoto Empire

ETHIOPIA

SLAVE COAST

Old Calabar

East Africa

BIGHT OF BIAFRA

Congo Basin

CONGO RIVER

LAKE TANGANYIKA

Zanzibar

INDIAN OCEAN

ATLANTIC OCEAN

The Practice of Slavery

We know that slavery began in Africa centuries ago, but because African societies did not leave written histories, piecing together the past is like detective work. The clues are bits of pottery, coins, gold and other metals, pieces of cloth, the remains of buildings, the records of travelers.

Al-Yaqubi, an Arab geographer who lived in the late ninth century, gives one of the first written reports of slave trading within Africa: "I have been informed," he writes, "that kings of the blacks sell their own people without justification or in consequence of war."

For centuries, Africans made raids on their neighbors for slaves to trade. The raiders were considered to be heroes, as in this old song about the ruler of a kingdom in Central Africa who made an enemy warrior flee, and captured his followers:

> Again and again you put him to flight,
>
> then forced him onto a raft of papyrus grass, . . .
>
> and captured [from his following] a thousand slaves,
>
> and took them and scattered them in the open places of Bagirmi.
>
> The best you took [and sent home] as the first fruits of battle.
>
> The children crying on their mothers you snatched away from their mothers.
>
> You took the slave wife from a slave,
>
> and set them in lands far removed from one another.

Another account of African slavery comes from Ibn Battuta, a Muslim from the north coast of Africa who traveled the world between 1325 and 1354. His book, *The Journey*, gives us a glimpse of slavery in Africa before the Europeans arrived. At Takadda, an oasis in the Sahara desert, the traders "vie with one another in the number of slaves and servants they have," he writes. He tells us that the slaves worked in the copper mines and smelted the copper in their houses. The copper was turned into a kind of money, and it was used to buy meat and firewood – and slaves. He even gave the slaves a backhanded compliment: "From this country are brought beautiful slave women and eunuchs and heavy fabrics." Ibn Battuta left Takadda in a caravan that included six hundred slave women.

Regional Differences

What would your life have been like if you had been a slave in Africa? That depends on where you lived. In the Sahara, the camel-riding nomads had little use for slaves except to guard the unfortunate captives being transported across the desert in caravans, or to grow dates in desert oases. In more fertile areas like the highlands around the Great Lakes of East Africa, and the grassy savannas south of the Sahara, women slaves hoed the fields. In West Africa, slaves worked in the gold mines. Farther north, entire slave villages produced the food that fed the Songhay kingdom's armies.

Along the Congo River system, with its active trading network for metal goods, few slaves were needed. In southern Africa there was a long-standing rivalry between Tswana farmer-herders, who had chiefs and kept slaves, and San hunter-gatherers, who did not have enough people to support a slave class. The Tswana would capture San children and keep them as servants unless their parents ransomed them with cattle.

Slave Work

In some African societies, families had only a few slaves who were part of the household, working side by side with family members and even eating their meals with them. As time went on, a household slave's children might be accepted as members of the society, slaves no longer.

In larger communities where three out of every four people might be slaves, life was much different. Slaves lived in slave villages (some with slave chiefs) on the outskirts of a settlement, worked in groups, and neither ate nor worked with their masters. A form of sharecropping (sharing the crop between landlord and laborer) evolved in some regions. In the early nineteenth century in the Sokoto Empire, the master gave his slave a wife and fed the slave until the harvest. The slave worked five days a week from morning until midday, and then was free to work his portion of the land for himself. At harvest, the master gave him extra grain. In the dry season, slaves repaired houses, rebuilt fences, and even raided enemy villages for the master.

In parts of Africa where slaves made up the ruler's army, outstanding slave soldiers might be appointed officers, government administrators, trade representatives, even diplomats. A ruler might also accumulate a large number of slaves to show off; the more slaves you had, the richer and more powerful you were.

Slave Sacrifices

Like the Arab traveler who witnessed a slave girl being sacrificed by her Viking owners in the tenth century, a Portuguese navigator reported watching slave sacrifices in Senegambia (today's Senegal and Gambia) five hundred years ago. As late as the nineteenth century, when former slaves began to record their experiences, they talked about their fear of being sacrificed.

Msatulwa Mwachitete was captured when he was a child in East Africa in 1891. Years later, in Tanzania, he told the story of his life to a Christian missionary who wrote it down for him.

As a young man, Msatulwa was a bodyguard and butler to the sister of the chief. Although he was well fed and well treated, he yearned to go home. His brother also lived as a slave in the chiefdom, and though Msatulwa thought about running away, he was afraid the chief might kill or sell his brother if he did. Fearing that the two of them might be sacrificed, he begged his brother to escape with him:

> I thought, "Here are we, two slaves, alone in this country. My brothers and sisters and relations have all been sold. Some of them have been sacrificed to the ancestors on the graves of chiefs. Why should we stay in this country?" And then I thought, "One day Mkoma [the chief] will die, and they will come and kill us, that we may die with him. We shall be sacrificed, for there are no other slaves. We alone are left." For it is a custom . . . on the death of the chief to bury four people with him: one of the elders, one of his wives, and two slaves – a man and a woman. They are strangled and their throats cut so that the blood flows into the grave, in which they are all buried with the dead chief. The body of the chief is placed on the knee of the wife, and she holds him in her arms. These people are to look after the chief and to serve him in the land of the shadows. . . . There are other sacrifices, too. When a new chief comes to the throne and goes to pray at the grave of the dead chief, another man is sacrificed. He is killed on the grave like a sheep or an ox. This is the sacrifice to ancestors.

This wooden carving for the funeral of an African man shows that he was such a successful trader that he could afford a European-style hat, jacket, and flintlock gun.

At last he happened to meet his uncle in a caravan. Here was the chance he'd been waiting for! He convinced his brother to flee with him, and they made their escape at night, arriving home nine and a half years after being captured.

After the Europeans Arrived

African slaves had been traded to Europe at times — for instance, to work in Italy after the plague. But what we think of as the European slave trade began with the Portuguese. When they were sent to explore the west coast of Africa by Prince Henry the Navigator in the 1400s, they found a thriving slave trade. One of Prince Henry's captains reported that a king who ruled the Senegambia region

> supports himself by raids which result in many slaves from his own as well as neighboring countries. He employs these slaves in cultivating the land allotted to him: but he also sells many to Saharan Muslim traders in return for horses and other goods, and also to the Christians, since they have begun to trade with these blacks.

By 1448, the Portuguese were trading with African merchants who exchanged a thousand slaves for horses, silver, and silks, items that the chiefs of Mali, Songhay, and other local kingdoms craved.

The sixteenth century was a time of exploration for Europeans. The Dutch, the English, and the French followed the Portuguese to Africa and later across the Atlantic. Maps were drawn and redrawn, and untold riches in the form of gold and silver, sugar, tobacco, and rice were suddenly within reach. The Europeans wanted slaves to help them reap those riches. Since slave trading and slave raiding were already in place in Africa, the Europeans could get all the human merchandise they wanted.

The port of Old Calabar, on the Bight of Biafra — a large bay on the West African coast of today's Nigeria — was just one of many trading centers. The merchants of Old Calabar controlled the slave trade on the Cross River. When a European ship arrived at the river's mouth, it stopped and fired its cannon. Once the Europeans had paid *comey* (customs duty) to the Africans, a native boat escorted the ship upriver. The Africans then set off with their fleets of canoes, each paddled by forty to fifty slaves, to pick up their human cargo.

Dotted along the riverbank were small villages, easy pickings for the raiders. The slavers loaded twenty or thirty captives into the canoe, arms tied behind their backs with twigs and grass ropes. Once the canoes landed downstream, the captives were taken to the houses of African traders who fed them and oiled their skin to make them look healthier. Then they called in the Europeans, who inspected the group before shunting them once more into canoes which took them to the ships that would transport them to the Americas. The traders didn't care if they tore husband from wife, or children from their parents' arms.

The Africans were paid with European goods, including muskets. This was the beginning of a vicious cycle: the more guns the Africans had, the easier it was for them to raid villages, the larger their haul of slaves grew, and the more guns they could acquire. The number of slaves transported from Old Calabar doubled every ten years from 1700 to 1750, making slave traders there immensely rich and powerful.

The growth of the slave trade caused tragic social changes. Before the Europeans came, the oldest member, or "father of the house," was the head of the community. Now money became more valuable than the traditional wisdom of the elders, and the leader was the richest member, or "father of the canoe." Such men were often slave owners. The traditional social order fell apart.

Another change was even more deadly: warfare between clans increased. In the 1760s, two rival clans were competing for control of the slave trade in the Old Calabar region, slowing the supply of slaves. The English, who favored one of the clans, set off a war between them. The victorious clan took over the trade on the river, and the flow of captives resumed.

Old Calabar's story was repeated throughout the continent. From 1450 to 1900 the slave trade robbed Africa of its workers, warfare and slave raids accelerated, and at least twelve million human beings were shipped away to the Americas.

The Slave Trade Survives

Even when the British and American slave trade ended in the early nineteenth century, slavery did not end in Africa. Why? One reason was that Europeans had a growing appetite for African products like peanuts and palm oil (used in making soap), and that increased the use of slave labor within Africa. Besides, the states that had grown rich on the slave trade became weaker when it ended. The results were

---

THE LONG SHADOW

In the Cross River region, not all captives were exported across the Atlantic. Africans kept some of them to work as slaves. Today, people there avoid using the word "slave" when they talk about the past. But memories are long; they know who is descended from free people, and who from slaves. In the past, slaves were housed in *etek asung*, "slave villages" on the outskirts of a community; today, descendants of slaves still live in separate communities. They are not allowed to take part in the Etokobi dance, a ritual performed at the funerals of important people. And to this day, when a new chief is to be selected, tensions rise, since by custom the position cannot be filled by any descendant of a former slave.

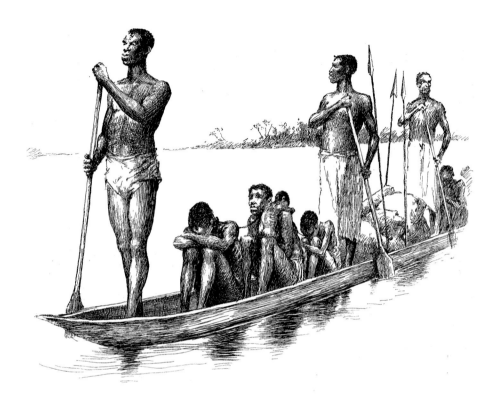

The passengers in this dugout canoe are victims of a slave raid in the Congo in the 1880s.

disastrous for their people. Bands of Islamic peasants and herders in West Africa declared a jihad and formed armies to conquer one weakened state after another. By the end of the nineteenth century, the Sokoto caliphate (a territory under a Muslim religious leader) in today's Nigeria, had become one of the largest slave societies in modern history, with as many as two and a half million slaves.

Slavery lasted in many parts of Africa, not only those that had been directly part of the Atlantic slave trade. On the other side of the continent, in Ethiopia, slavery was practiced throughout the nineteenth century. When slave prices were low, even poor peasants in the north could afford slaves to help them work their land. In southern Africa, the Tswana people sold their San enemies to white settlers as farm laborers. The San's low status lasted well into the twentieth century.

Slave raiding laid waste to whole regions of Africa. The southern end of Tanganyika, once "peopled with large and prosperous villages," had become a desolate wasteland with "not a solitary human being – nothing but burned houses and bleaching skeletons," wrote a traveler in 1888.

KING LEOPOLD'S SLAVE KINGDOM

King Leopold II of Belgium wanted an African colony for his country and great wealth for himself. Public opinion in Europe and the United States was strongly antislavery, and around 1876 he convinced powerful Europeans that Belgium could end the African slave trade by developing the Congo through building roads, a railroad, and trading posts, and encouraging Christian missionaries. Once he was recognized as "Sovereign and Protector" of the Congo, Leopold changed his tune. He used the Congo's riches – ivory and rubber – to fill his own pockets by enslaving the Congolese people.

Leopold called his kingdom the Congo Free State, but it was anything but free. At the trading posts his private company set up, natives were forced to provide fish, meat, and vegetables to Leopold's traders. Armed white officers surrounded African villages and held women and children hostage to force the men into the forests to harvest rubber. Workers who refused or did not meet the rubber quota would be beaten, or even have their hands cut off. Uncooperative villages were burned. The toll of this abuse was huge; by some estimates, as much as half the Congo's population died between 1885 and 1908, murdered, weakened by disease and malnutrition, or worked to death.

Bit by bit, news of what was happening in the Congo leaked out. Black American journalist George Washington Williams witnessed the atrocities firsthand, and boldly accused Leopold of sponsoring slavery. "The labor force at the stations of your Majesty's Government in the Upper River is composed of slaves of all ages and both sexes," he wrote. By 1908, Leopold was in disgrace. He turned over his personal state to the Belgian government. Belgium continued to control the rubber industry. Although it put an end to the mutilations and hostage-taking, and even prohibited slavery, it kept the workers in slavelike conditions for decades to come.

Many Congolese workers were brutally punished if they failed to harvest enough rubber to please the Belgian rubber companies. The hands of Mola, who is seated, were bound too tightly; he lost them both to gangrene. Yoka's hand was deliberately amputated.

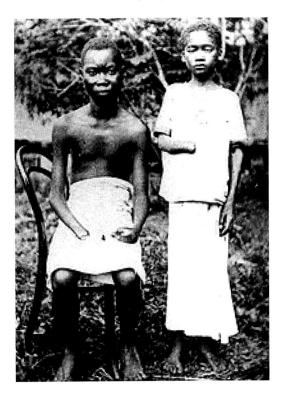

Colonization

At first Europeans were drawn to Africa for the riches it could supply, but by the second half of the nineteenth century they began to move in. The age of colonization had begun. Though their countryfolk back in Europe were against slavery, many colonists were afraid to upset local people by tampering with their traditional way of life, which relied on slaves and slave trading. The colonists and their African allies sometimes joined forces. For example, in 1848 France abolished slavery, meaning that the slaves in France's island colonies of St-Louis and Gorée, in today's Senegal, were freed. But rather than helping the ex-slaves build a new life, French authorities in those colonies expelled them to the mainland as "vagabonds."

Today, although slavery is no longer legal in Africa, far too many people can still tell their own stories of being slaves. The final chapter of the long saga of African slavery has not been written.

THE TALE OF MELI

Meli was just five years old when warriors captured her in what is now Zambia. She and other captives were forced to march for miles, carrying chickens, cooking pots, and other loot from their devastated village. If a mother collapsed, too exhausted to keep carrying the heavy loads and her baby, the marauders tied the baby up into a bundle and hung the child from a tree to starve. To them, chickens and cooking pots were worth more than children.

Years later, Meli told the story of her terrible experience to her son. "Hunger said, '[I'll be] wherever you go!'" she told him.

Our captors wondered how to feed such a large crowd. Their leader said, "Roast maize for them to chew." They roasted the maize and beans but gave us only beans. You should have heard the sounds that we made: *kukutu, kukutu, kukutu.* We sounded like goats chewing maize. After we finished eating our beans, thirst also said, "[I'll be] wherever you go!" We asked for water. They said, "Where have you seen water? You may as well drink your own urine." We spent the night with dry throats.

Meli's first owner was a man who put her to work drying harvested grain by the fire. Chilled by the damp cold, she threw extra wood on the fire. A spark set the hut ablaze:

I shouted, "Help! The hut is on fire!"

The man and his wife were furious and they scolded me very strongly. The husband, mad with rage, seized me and almost threw me into the fire. But, thank God, the woman objected strongly, saying, "Do not bring evil upon us. Don't you know that this person belongs to a chief's family?"

The man said, "You have been saved! But from now on you will eat only wild things you find yourself."

Meli became too sick to work, so her owner threw her into a pit to die. She was saved from starvation by a little boy who brought her bits of pumpkin to eat. She recovered, only to be sold again and again until she ended up in a strange village.

There she heard a rumor that white men had ordered an end to slave trading. But before she could learn whether that was true, she became sick again and was sold to Arab traders who marched her away with their other slaves. As they traveled, one brave man offered to show the Arabs a route that would let them avoid the white men, who were on the lookout for slave traders. The Arabs gave him permission to survey the route. He went straight to white officials and told them everything, and they set a trap for the slavers.

Early the next morning the horn sounded telling us to tie up our bundles. The second horn sounded, signifying departure time. . . . After a short while we heard gunshots. Everybody was scared and jumped and scattered into the bush. What confusion! . . . I went to the anthill where I found a little boy, hidden. He said, "Hide your head in the elephant grass. Get down. Don't let them see us." As I was stooping, another child joined us.

The children remained hidden, not realizing that the shots were aimed at the Arabs. When the shooting stopped, they had no idea where they were or whom to trust. All they knew was that they were hungry. Eventually they made their way to a white Christian mission at a nearby village, where they saw a woman sitting and sewing.

We went up to her, greeted her, and sat nearby. . . . She said, ". . . we are very happy that you have arrived safely." As she talked to us I noticed that she had no toes. I drew Maci's attention and said, "Oh, look, she has no toes! Her foot is all smooth and round." My friend said, "Yes! Even those who sent us here had similar feet." Shortly after, the husband came and greeted us; he, too, had no toes! We then wondered how these people were made. Of course we realized later that they wore shoes.

Though Meli was reunited with her family, she stayed in the missionary world for the rest of her life.

CHAPTER 6
EXPLORERS, LABORERS, WARRIORS, CHIEFS: THE AMERICAS

Christopher Columbus set sail in 1492 to find a westerly route by sea to the "Indies" in the East, the source of precious spices, gold, and boundless riches. Instead, he landed in the Bahamas, not far from Florida. He'd stumbled upon a place most Europeans did not know existed.

When Columbus and his crew came ashore, both the Europeans and the native people were amazed by what they saw. Columbus described his impressions in his journal. We will never know if he interpreted the North Americans' behavior correctly, but he wrote that the Europeans looked otherworldly to the natives because they had never before seen white people, not to mention people wearing pantaloons and doublets. And though the Spaniards came on ships, the native people thought they had descended from the heavens. Columbus can't have understood their language, but he claimed that they shouted, "Come! Come! See the people from the sky!"

Columbus called the natives Indians because he thought he was in the Indies. This artist imagines him meeting them and offering them cheap trinkets.

The natives looked equally exotic to the Europeans. Columbus wrote, "They went naked, men and women, as their mothers bore them, except that some women cover one place only with the leaf of a plant or with a net of cotton which they make for that." He described them as generous and hospitable and said they had all greeted the Europeans "so that not one, big or little, remained behind, and all brought something to eat and drink, which they gave with marvelous love."

Columbus may have admired the American natives, but everywhere he traveled – from as far north as the Bahamas, through the Caribbean, and into Honduras and Panama – he looked on every person he met as a potential slave. Although they vastly outnumbered the Europeans, he knew that he could capture them easily. He and his crew had guns and steel knives and swords. The natives did not.

In 1494 Columbus wrote to King Ferdinand and Queen Isabella of Spain, "Whenever Your Highnesses may command, all of them [natives] can be taken to Castile or held captive in this same island; because with 50 men all of them could be held in subjection and can be made to do whatever one might wish." The royal couple told Columbus not to resort to slavery, but he had found no other valuables to send to Spain. In 1495 he captured about 1,600 Taino people in Hispaniola (now the Dominican Republic and Haiti). Of them, 500 men and women were loaded onto ships for sale in Spain. He let the Spaniards who were staying behind choose slaves for themselves from among the remaining Tainos.

The kidnapped natives suffered terribly on the voyage. By the time they reached Spain, only three hundred were still alive, and half of those were ill. The survivors were sold in Seville, but most of them died soon after they landed.

Columbus took slaves, but he did not bring the idea of slavery to the Americas. It was already there. The "Indians," as he called them, were not one single people. From the northernmost points of North America to the southernmost points of South America, and east to west across the continents, lived people with different languages, religions, physical characteristics, and ways of life. For hundreds of years before and after Columbus's arrival, they captured one another for use as slaves.

The Tupinamba of Brazil

The Tupinamba people, who lived in what is now Brazil, practiced both slavery and human sacrifice. Their huge thatched houses, built around a central plaza, could accommodate two hundred people, with special areas for the heads of

DEFEATING THROUGH DISEASE

Far more native people were killed by the Europeans' diseases than by their weapons. Smallpox was common in Europe at that time, and people who did not die from it developed immunity to it. The disease was unknown in the Americas until the Spaniards arrived. Many historians believe that smallpox killed most of the Tainos of Hispaniola between 1494 and 1496. No one knows exactly how many Tainos there were when Columbus first arrived – perhaps as many as five hundred thousand. By the year 1540, only five hundred remained. Smallpox and other diseases, such as typhus and influenza, had ravaged the native population throughout North and South America. Smallpox had killed about half the Aztec population in Mexico, for example, and wiped out many of the Incas of South America.

families, their relatives, and slaves they'd captured in war. Although the slaves lived in their masters' homes, the Tupinamba always considered them outsiders. Even though some slaves lived with their masters for years, every slave knew what was coming: death in a horrible religious ritual.

Until that day, the Tupinamba tried to keep their slaves healthy and happy, and at times even found wives for the men. But they could also be very cruel: they tied ropes around their slaves' necks, decorated with one bead for each month the slaves had left to live.

The sacrifice ritual lasted several days. First, they teased the slave by letting him or her try to escape. When they caught the victim, which they always did, they performed an elaborate ritual that included dancing and singing. They decorated the slave and chose one Tupinamba to club the slave to death. Afterward, the body was dismembered and roasted, and the victim's flesh was eaten. The heads of the victims were displayed on poles.

The Aztecs

The Aztecs had a powerful, complex empire that controlled central and southern Mexico from the fourteenth to the sixteenth century. People were divided into three classes – noble, commoner, and slave – and slaves were bought and sold in a marketplace near today's Mexico City. Slavery was not hereditary, and often it was not even permanent. Children of slaves were born free.

Aztecs had strict rules about slaves who sold themselves to pay debts. An owner who was dissatisfied with a slave and wanted to sell the person to someone else had to ask the slave's permission. But the owner could sell the slave if he had witnesses who had seen him scold the slave for bad behavior, and if the scolding had not changed the slave's behavior. If a slave had been sold three times, the last owner could sell him for sacrifice.

The Aztecs' most important god was Huitzilopochtli, a sun god. They believed that he needed sacrificial blood to rise in the morning. Slaves who were sacrificed were usually men, and were often debtor slaves or slaves from foreign lands.

The People of the Totem Pole

The northwest coast of North America, from Alaska to northern California, was home to several nations that were often at war with one another. The Tlingit of

At the top of a massive stepped pyramid, this Aztec priest is cutting out the heart of a living person, most likely a slave, as a sacrifice to the god Huitzilopochtli.

southeast Alaska and the Haida of the Queen Charlotte Islands raided one another for women and children. The Nootka encouraged the nations who lived around what is now Vancouver to fight one another so they could buy up the survivors. Only Nootka kings and chiefs could own slaves. Europeans asked one chief if he would like to go to England. He said no. "I have slaves who hunt for me, paddle me in my canoe, and have my wife to attend me. Why should I care to leave?" In England he would have to work.

Throughout the northwest owners traded their slaves, so that many ended up far from home. A slave's relative could buy the person back, but ransom was expensive. Besides, there was such shame attached to being a slave that family members usually did not want their relative returned.

Slaves, male and female, often lived in their owners' homes and did the same tasks that free people did. They fetched water, collected firewood, made cloth and cleaned pelts, built and paddled canoes, and hunted and fished. But the fear of being sacrificed must have been ever present.

A PERILOUS ADVENTURE

An Englishman who wanted adventure was sure to find it by working on a sailing ship. John R. Jewitt got more excitement than he had bargained for as a twenty-year-old blacksmith on the trading ship *Boston*. In 1803, when the ship anchored in Nootka Sound, near Vancouver Island, Jewitt saw native people for the first time. For several days the Nootka and their king, Maquina, came on board, bringing salmon and other supplies for the sailors and leaving with small gifts. Everything seemed to go well until the tenth day, when the Nootka attacked the ship, killing all the crew except Jewitt and John Thompson, a sailmaker. Jewitt later wrote:

But what a terrific spectacle met my eyes; six naked savages, standing in a circle around me, covered with the blood of my murdered comrades, with their daggers uplifted in their hands, prepared to strike. I now thought my last moment had come, and recommended my soul to my Maker.

Maquina proposed a deal. He would spare Jewitt's life if the Englishman agreed to be his slave, fight for him in his battles, repair his muskets, and make daggers and knives for him. Jewitt readily agreed. Thompson had hidden during the attack, and when the Nootka discovered him hours later, Jewitt convinced Maquina to spare his life by claiming that the sailmaker was his father. The pair joined more than fifty male and female slaves Maquina owned. The slaves lived in the same house as the master, and —

are usually kindly treated, eat of the same food, and live as well as their masters. They are compelled however at times to labour severely, as not only all the menial offices are performed by them, such as bringing water, cutting wood and a variety of others, but they are obliged to make the canoes, to assist in building and repairing the houses, to supply their masters with fish and to attend them to war and to fight for them. . . . The females are employed principally in manufacturing cloth, in cooking, collecting berries, &c. and with regard to food and living in general have not a much harder lot than their mistresses.

The main difference was that the king could force the women to have children with any men he chose.

Jewitt protected himself by acting kindly toward his captors. He adopted their customs, remained cheerful, made ornaments for the women and fishhooks for the men, and learned their language. One of the more surprising duties Maquina gave him and Thompson was to guard him at night with guns and cutlasses, "being apparently afraid to trust any of his own men." More than two years after their capture, another American vessel came to Nootka Sound, and Jewitt and Thompson escaped.

Sacrifices were sometimes part of elaborate ceremonies called potlatches. The word *potlatch* means "giving" — a chief displayed his power and wealth to another chief by giving away his possessions. Potlatches were held to mark important occasions like births, deaths, marriages, or victories over enemies. A chief could become impoverished by his potlatch, but he would expect to get rich again from the next one he attended as a guest.

Guests arrived at potlatches in decorated canoes, wearing their best clothes. Hosts served a sumptuous feast, and sometimes there was dancing and singing, but the main focus was gift-giving. Records show that chiefs might offer as many as 54 dressed elk skins, 8 canoes, 2,000 silver bracelets, 7,000 brass bracelets, 33,000 blankets, and 6 slaves. The slaves who were given away as gifts were fortunate, because occasionally a slave was felled by the chief with a special club called a "slave killer," as a way for the chief to show off his power.

The Iroquois

The Iroquois were a confederation of five nations — the Mohawk, the Oneida, the Onondaga, the Cayuga, and the Seneca — that banded together in the sixteenth century. The Tuscarora joined the confederacy around 1720, and by that time Iroquois territory reached from the Carolinas into Canada along the east coast. Their confederation has been called the world's oldest democracy, with a council made up of elected chiefs from each nation.

The Iroquois were skilled fighters in both large-scale wars and smaller skirmishes. Slavery rarely followed the large wars; instead, defeated enemies were massacred, tortured, or sacrificed. The Iroquois more commonly captured slaves in their "mourning" wars, small attacks aimed at seizing people to replace members of their own community who had died. Captives were stripped of their original names, and much worse. "As soon as they have taken a prisoner, they cut off his fingers; they tear his shoulders and his back with a knife; they bind him with very tight binds," wrote a Jesuit priest who witnessed an Iroquois attack in the seventeenth century. The Iroquois killed the most badly mutilated captives, and kept the others as slaves to tend fields and carry heavy packs, including the warriors' food.

Whenever they could, Iroquois women depended on slaves to do all their chores. The mother of a Seneca woman worried that her dead daughter could not manage in heaven without her slaves. She asked the Jesuit priest who had baptized her daughter to convert an ill slave to Christianity so that, when the slave died, she would go to heaven, where she could serve the daughter. The mother said:

> [My daughter] was a mistress here and commanded more than twenty slaves, who are still with me; she knew not what it was to go to the forest to get wood, or the River to draw water; she could not take upon herself the care of all that has to do with domestic duties. Now I have no doubt that, being at present the only one of our family in Paradise, she has great difficulty in getting used to it; for she will be obliged to do her own cooking, to go for wood and water, and to do everything with her own hands in the preparation of her food and drink.

The Iroquois nation waned after years of fighting the Europeans, and many of their members left to join the Catholic mission villages. The slave system fell apart and eventually disappeared.

Slaves of the Europeans

Despite the wishes of King Ferdinand and Queen Isabella, Columbus forced the native people in Hispaniola to work for the Spaniards. Under a system called *encomienda*, natives could only work if they paid their masters for the privilege, usually by giving them some of the gold they mined or the crops they grew. In return, the masters were supposed to protect the workers. Although this system often left the workers with nothing, it received the blessing of King Ferdinand in 1503 and spread throughout the Americas. In some places *encomienda* did not end until the seventeenth century.

While the Spanish were settling the Caribbean Islands, the Portuguese were laying claim to Brazil. As early as 1500, they were taking Africans there as slaves. In 1505, a year after Queen Isabella's death, the Spanish imported Africans to work in the copper mines of Hispaniola. By 1510, King Ferdinand had approved the use of African slaves in the island's gold mines.

The introduction of African slavery did not end the enslavement of the native people. Spanish law said that they could only be kept as slaves if they were captured in a "just war." There was a catch: the king considered a war "just" if the native people refused to accept him and his daughter as their sovereigns and refused to become Catholic. The result was that Spaniards could call almost any slave raid a just war.

But natives were proving to be unsatisfactory slaves. They knew the land and could escape and disappear – unlike the Africans, whose skin color marked them as runaways. And they fell ill from the terrible labor forced on them and from diseases they caught from the Europeans.

The hardships they suffered troubled some Spaniards, most famously Bartolomé de Las Casas. Originally a planter with natives working for him and paying *encomienda*, Las Casas had become a priest. By 1514 he was so appalled by the mistreatment of the natives that he rejected the practice of *encomienda* and fought for the natives' welfare. The Spaniards, he wrote, "came with their horsemen and armed with sword and lance, making most cruel havocs and slaughters," sparing no infant, mother, or child. Las Casas journeyed five or six times to Spain to plead for laws to protect the native people. In time he became known as the "protector of the Indians."

In 1550, Las Casas took part in a debate about slavery. His opponent argued that the native people "require, by their own nature and in their own interests, to be placed under the authority of civilized and virtuous princes or nations, so that they may learn, from the might, wisdom, and law of their conquerors, to practice better morals, worthier customs and a more civilized way of life." Las Casas spoke from his experience with them, explaining that native people were devout and hard workers. "Mankind is one, and all men are alike in that which concerns their creation," he said. The debate did not settle the question, but the treatment of native slaves slowly improved. Three years later the Spanish king prohibited their enslavement, but the practice continued.

Although Las Casas was a tireless champion of fair treatment of native people, he did not speak out against all slavery. In fact, he urged that native slaves be replaced by Africans. Many Europeans

Bartolomé de Las Casas, now a priest, looks out a window at the native people whose enslavement he denounced. He also wrote a history of the native people and their lives.

had seen natives dying under forced labor, and thought the Africans had more stamina and more experience farming. They also thought that the Africans in the New World did not suffer from enslavement the way native people did. By 1540, approximately ten thousand Africans a year were being transported to the Americas to live and die in slavery.

Long after Las Casas's death in 1566, his writings revealed that he had had second thoughts about enslaving Africans. He wrote, "It is as unjust to enslave Negroes as Indians and for the same reasons." Unfortunately, his words came too late to do any good. As native slavery diminished, African slavery expanded. It was to envelop four continents for hundreds of years.

CHAPTER 7
THE TREACHEROUS TRIANGLE: SOUTH AMERICA AND THE CARIBBEAN

Before he became a slave, Mahommah Gardo Baquaqua had never seen a white man, a ship, or the ocean. He could not have imagined what a dreadful fate awaited him.

Baquaqua was born in what is now Benin, on the west coast of Africa. Years later, he described the horror of being a "poor, unfortunate, miserable wretch" who had been sold away from everyone he knew and everything he loved and crowded in with strangers on a ship to await further heartache.

> We were thrust into the hold of the vessel in a state of nudity, the males on one side and the females on the other; the hold was so low that we could not stand up, but were obliged to crouch upon the floor or sit down; day and night were the same to us, sleep being denied us from the confined position of our bodies, and we became desperate through suffering and fatigue.

If a slave complained, Baquaqua said, "his flesh was cut with a knife, and pepper or vinegar was rubbed in to make him peaceable."

Between 1500 and 1870, more than eleven million Africans were torn from their families and homes and forced onto slave ships bound for South America and the Caribbean. Whether they were transported on a Portuguese ship like Baquaqua's, or on one owned by the Dutch, the Spanish, the British, the Danes, or the French, the captives crossed the Atlantic from Africa to the Americas on a voyage called the Middle Passage. The trip was called "middle" because the ships had a three-part route. First, they left European ports carrying goods like textiles, guns, and brandy to be exchanged in Africa for slaves. On the middle section of the trip, they left Africa with human cargo bound for the Americas, where the slaves were traded for sugar, rum, and other commodities. The third passage brought the ships and their new cargo back to their home ports in Europe. The triangle worked well because on each section the prevailing winds cooperated, blowing the cargo-laden ships clockwise along the route.

The title page of Mahommah Baquaqua's biography shows him in African dress and calls him a native of "Zoogoo" in the African interior. It notes that the book includes descriptions of "that part of the world including the manners and customs of the inhabitants." Although it was written by an Englishman, the story was narrated to the writer by Baquaqua himself.

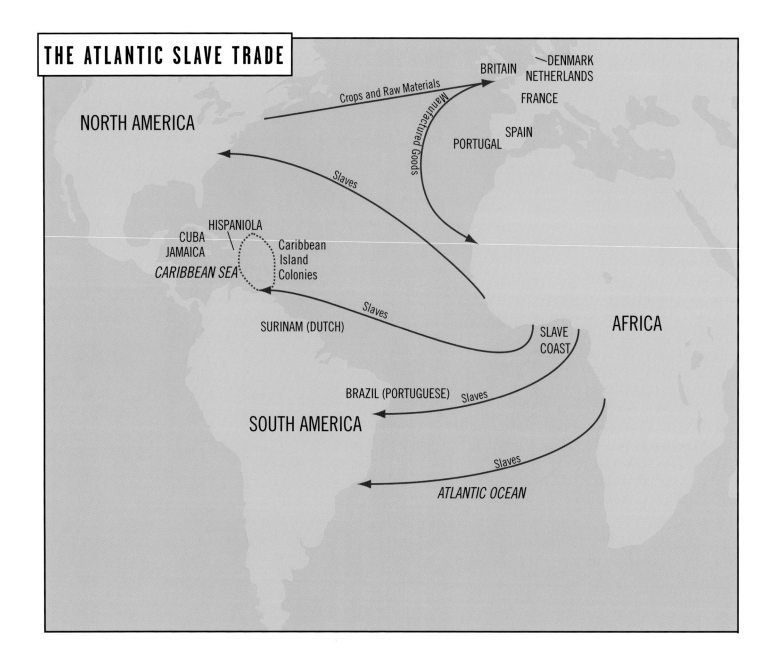

THE ATLANTIC SLAVE TRADE

NORTH AMERICA

BRITAIN
DENMARK
NETHERLANDS
FRANCE

SPAIN
PORTUGAL

Crops and Raw Materials

Manufactured Goods

Slaves

HISPANIOLA
CUBA
JAMAICA
Caribbean
Island
Colonies
CARIBBEAN SEA

Slaves

SURINAM (DUTCH)

SLAVE
COAST

AFRICA

BRAZIL (PORTUGUESE)   Slaves

SOUTH AMERICA

Slaves

ATLANTIC OCEAN

Slave ships varied in size, with smaller vessels carrying as few as 150 unfortunate victims in their holds, and larger ones cramming in more than 400. Ships often had removable platforms so that they could crowd on more people. The slaves shared the dreadful voyage with strangers from other villages. Even if they had no language or customs in common, they were united in their longing for their homes and families. They would find no comfort on the Middle Passage.

The Atlantic Slave Trade

Baquaqua's capture came in the closing years of the Atlantic slave trade, which had begun in the fifteenth century, when Europeans expected their new colonies in North and South America to make them rich. To succeed, they needed cheap workers, and they looked to Africa to supply them. The Portuguese captured and shipped more slaves than any other nation – more than five million people by the 1860s. Other European powers, including Britain, France, Holland, Denmark, and Spain, shipped about six million Africans to South America and the Caribbean.

The Voyage to America

In 1799, Sibell, a slave woman in Barbados, told her story to a white man who wrote it down exactly as she spoke, spelling words the way she pronounced them. "Me nebber see de White people before, me nebber see de great ships pon de water before, me nebber hear de Waves before which me frighten so much-ee dat me thought me would die."

Before European traders took slaves on board, they made them pass an inspection by a "surgeon." The slaves must have been terrified and humiliated as the doctor, a strange white man, made them take off their clothes and move naked in front of everyone, running, walking, and lifting and stretching their arms and legs. The surgeon's sole interest was to make sure they were healthy enough to survive the journey and attract buyers.

Slaves who were not accepted stayed with the African trader. An officer on the ship would name the price for those who passed inspection. European traders paid African traders not in money but in goods: textiles, guns and gunpowder, tobacco, rum, brandy, or other alcohol, or cowrie shells, which were used as money in West Africa.

FROM SLAVE TRADER TO SLAVE

Like other African traders in Old Calabar, the Robin Johns were black, could speak English, did business with Europeans, and even took British-sounding names. They were successful, but they had enemies.

In 1767 James Bivins, an English trader, tricked two members of the Robin John family, Little Ephraim and Ancona Robin, into boarding his ship, where the crew bound them in irons. The ship sailed away to the Caribbean island of Dominica, where Little Ephraim and Ancona became slaves. Their owner did not treat them badly, but they were determined to escape and return to Africa. After seven months, the captain of another British ship agreed to help them if they boarded his ship at night. Instead he took them to Virginia, then a British colony, where he sold them to yet another captain. That captain gave them a taste of the misery of slavery. It lasted for five years, until the captain died at sea.

Again Little Ephraim and Ancona found a captain who promised to return them to Africa if they came to his ship at night. They traveled with him to England, but they'd been fooled once more; he planned to send them back to Virginia for sale. Meanwhile, Little Ephraim wrote letters asking for help, and eventually he and Ancona were released by order of the court. No sooner were they free, however, than they were arrested for failing to pay for their voyage from Virginia!

Little Ephraim wrote to the chief justice of the British court, arguing that he and Ancona should be released because they were enslaved illegally. "There was not any war between the people of New Town and the people of Old Town, but only a quarrel or dispute about trade, which never occasioned any fighting," he argued. The judge ruled in their favor in November 1773, but it would be another year before they reached home.

The two were deeply in debt by the time they got back to Africa. In spite of all they had suffered as slaves, Little Ephraim felt he had no choice but to return to the slave trade. He needed the money.

Following the inspection, several crew members held each slave down while an assistant rubbed tallow on a spot on the captive's right shoulder or stomach or arm. The assistant placed a piece of greased paper over the spot while another member of the crew placed a red-hot iron on top of it to burn the owner's sign or name into the slave's flesh. The wound would take days to heal, and over time the skin would rise where the burn had been inflicted.

Slave voyages usually lasted months, and were miserable from beginning to end. The owners cared only about getting the slaves across the ocean as quickly and cheaply as possible, so they could sell them for a large profit. While the slaves suffered mightily, the crew lived in fear, knowing that they were outnumbered. In the eighteenth century it was not unusual for a ship to carry four hundred or more slaves and fewer than twenty crew members. The sailors were ever fearful of attack, and tried to protect themselves by keeping the male slaves chained and shackled.

Even when the slave traders forced slaves to "dance" on deck for exercise, the shackles often remained. Officers enforced the exercise with a cat-o'-nine-tails, a whip that had nine thongs of braided rope or rawhide. A surgeon on a British slave ship in 1789 described the scene:

> This was done by means of a Cat of Nine Tails with which they were driven about one among the other, one of their country drums beating at the same time. On these occasions they were compelled to sing, the Cat being brandished over them for that purpose. It was the business of the chief mate to dance the men, and of [myself] and the second mate to dance the women. The men could only jump up and rattle their chains, but the women . . . were driven among one another.

African men and women were kept apart. The women were not chained because the officers were not afraid of them, but their relative freedom did not make the voyage any easier for them. The ship's crew often raped them.

In their home countries, Africans were used to eating meals of seasoned meat, fish, and fresh fruit, but on ship they were served a bland porridge of fava beans, millet, peas, or manioc, a flour common in Central and South America. In 1729 an English surgeon wrote that slaves who refused the food were "abused by sailors, who beat and kick them to that degree that sometimes they never recover."

The "dance" was a degrading and joyless exercise forced upon captives to keep them healthy enough to bring a good price, but a French slave trader claimed it was "full of jollity and good humor." Perhaps, for the sailors watching and laughing, it was.

Baquaqua said he and the other captives were desperate for water but were given just two cups per day. Once, when a sailor brought them a bucket of water, a captive tried to grab a knife from him so that he could get more. The slave was taken away and never seen again. Baquaqua assumed he had been thrown overboard.

Sickness spread quickly through the crowded and filthy quarters, and many slaves died from severe diarrhea, smallpox, fevers, or scurvy. It's no wonder that in some ports, when a ship arrived, a health official would come on board to make sure the slaves were not carrying any contagious diseases that could spread on land. Estimates are that in the early years, two out of every ten slaves died on the Middle Passage. Eager to keep the slaves alive, ship owners improved conditions by the eighteenth century, but still one in ten died. Approximately one and a half million Africans were cast, dead or alive, into the sea from slave ships.

THE *ZONG*

Every slave voyage was nightmarish, but it would be hard to think of one that was worse than that of the *Zong*. The ship carried 440 slaves and 17 whites when it left Africa for Jamaica in 1781. After about two months, approximately 60 slaves and 7 whites had died, more were ill, and supplies were running low. A ship's owner and captain could only get rich from a journey if they had healthy slaves to sell. With so many dead and many more sick, the *Zong*'s captain, Luke Collingwood, knew he was facing a financial loss.

Collingwood ordered his crew to throw the sick slaves overboard, in hopes of collecting money on the insurance. The policy would pay up if cargo, including slaves, was discarded to save other cargo, but it would not pay for losses because of illness. Although at first Collingwood's chief mate balked, in the days that followed, the sailors threw 133 living slaves overboard.

When the ship returned to England, the insurance company refused to pay for this "lost" cargo. The case went to court — as an insurance case, not as murder — and the ship owners won and got their money.

On Land

Once a slave ship arrived at its destination, the captain wanted quick sales. The longer it took to sell the slaves, the more money he had to spend on feeding and housing them. Baquaqua wrote about the scramble that took place as soon as a slave ship docked in Brazil:

> Down come all those that are interested in the arrival of the vessel with its cargo of living merchandize, who select from the stock those most suited to their different purposes, and purchase the slaves precisely in the same way that oxen or horses would be purchased in a market; but if there are not the kind of slaves in the one cargo, suited to the wants and wishes of the slave buyers, an order is given to the Captain for the particular sort required, which are furnished to order the next time the ship comes into port. Great numbers make quite a business of this buying and selling human flesh.

Baquaqua was sold to a man who owned four other slaves. His owner treated him like a beast of burden, requiring him to carry heavy rocks over long distances. "I was compelled to carry them that were so heavy it took three men to raise them upon my head," he said. At times a rock "would press so hard upon my head that I was obliged to throw it down upon the ground."

Baquaqua's master had a quick temper and did not hesitate to beat his slaves whenever he felt like it, even during the family's prayers. The Roman Catholic Church required that slaves be baptized, and let them attend Mass and confession. When the family and slaves came together to pray, Baquaqua said, "my master held a whip in his hand, and those who showed signs of inattention or drowsiness, were immediately brought to consciousness by a smart application of the whip." Baquaqua eventually became a Christian, but that was long after he left this owner.

In despair, Baquaqua tried to drown himself. He was rescued and returned to his master, who smashed him against the doorpost to punish him. That owner sold him to a dealer, and in time he was sent to sea as a slave for a ship's captain and his wife. They were as brutal as his first owner. When the ship docked in New York, Baquaqua escaped. With help, he made his way to Canada and finally became a free man, ten long years after he was captured in Africa.

Slaves in Agriculture

During the first years of the slave trade, white servants and African slaves did the same jobs. By the mid–1600s, slaves did all the household chores, including bathing and dressing their owners, carrying them in hammocks and sedan chairs, toting crates and water, making jewelry, weaving cloth, and even painting, sculpting, and making music.

But most slaves did farmwork. On plantations growing coffee, cotton, cocoa, and sugar, slaves worked hard, slept little, and ate poorly. On one coffee plantation they were awakened at three o'clock in the morning, long before the sun rose, and sent back to their quarters at nine at night or later, long after the sun had set. Many plantation owners did not care if they worked their slaves to death; one said he would get his money's worth if a slave lasted a year.

Slaves often made several visits a day to the community fountain to get water for the household's use. There they had a chance to talk with other slaves, though they might be under the watchful eye of a police officer, like the one who is breaking up a fight in this picture of slaves in Brazil.

The Bitter Business of Sugar

If any single crop was responsible for the growth of slavery in Brazil and the Caribbean, it was sugar. The Portuguese had already put blacks to work on their sugar plantations off the coast of Africa, and they did the same in Brazil. People in Europe were buying as much sugar as the Portuguese could sell, and with Brazil's warm climate the Portuguese expected to grow a lot more. They started their first sugar mills in Brazil in the 1530s, and by about 1640 they had shipped half a million African slaves there. Soon the Dutch, British, French, and Spanish established their own plantations throughout the Caribbean.

By the eighteenth century, many European planters had become so rich from sugar that they moved back to Europe and left white managers in charge of their plantations. One planter who stayed offers us a remarkable record of what life must have been like on his plantation on the French island of Martinique. Pierre Dessalles worried constantly about money and fretted about his slaves and his staff. In a letter dated July 1823, he wrote that twelve slaves had died since January, and he expected more deaths since thirty or forty more were ill. "I keep up my

A WOMAN'S STORY

Mary Prince was born to a slave in Bermuda around 1788. She was sold away from her family when she was twelve because her owner could no longer afford to keep her. In the years that followed, she had several masters. Prince never learned to write, so she described both the terrors and the joys of her life in a story that she dictated after she was free.

One of her most grueling jobs was extracting salt from the ocean and loading it onto vessels.

I was given a half barrel and a shovel, and had to stand up to my knees in the water, from four o'clock in the morning till nine, when we were given some Indian corn boiled in water, which we were obliged to swallow as fast as we could for fear the rain should come on and melt the salt. We were then called again to our tasks, and worked through the heat of the day; the sun flaming upon our heads like fire, and raising salt blisters in those parts which were not completely covered. Our feet and legs, from standing in the salt water for so many hours, soon became full of dreadful boils, which eat down in some cases to the very bone, afflicting the sufferers with great torment. We came home at twelve; ate our corn soup, called *blawly*,

courage although I am often quite dejected. What a terrible occupation I am engaged in! Yet I have to do it, the interest of my children demands it."

Although Dessalles felt wretched himself, he could not understand despair in his slaves. After two recently arrived slaves hanged themselves, he sounded bewildered about why they would be unhappy, or why other slaves would care about their deaths. In a letter to his mother, he wrote:

Nobody had done anything to them; they were having a perfectly gay and amiable time. Things are none the worse for it on the plantation. The Negroes were very sad about this event, but I harangued them and they recovered their good spirits. I do not have one of them sick in the hospital. Since one cannot hope to be ever tranquil in this business we are in, I just decided to put up with it.

Still, Dessalles thought he was a good master, and in some ways he was better than others. He made sure the slaves had three meals a day, disapproved when they were not given enough time to eat their lunch, and was even willing to listen to their side in a dispute. Once, a slave ran off with her daughter without any explanation. When they were found, he asked what had prompted her to leave. He wrote in his diary: "She replied that when Monsieur Jules [Dessalles's son] had taken away part of her time for lunch, she had become exasperated. I agreed not to do anything to her, but I warned her that, at the first infraction, I would not miss her." He appears to be saying that he will sell her if she ever runs off again.

Other owners were more heartless. By considering slaves less than human, they could treat them viciously with a clear conscience. Many of them shared the sentiments of Edward Long, an English planter in Jamaica who said that blacks were a different species from whites. He described African slaves as "unjust, cruel, barbarous, half-human, treacherous, deceitful thieves, drunkards, proud, lazy, unclean, shameless, jealous to fury, and cowards." We can only guess how many of those slaves would have described their owners the same way.

Slaves in Sugar Production

Plantations ranged in size, and as many as four hundred slaves worked on them. They labored from dawn to dusk during the harvest season, from January until

July. An overseer was always ready with a whip or other instrument of torture to punish anyone who did not seem to be working hard enough.

Plantation owners depended on the slaves for each step that converted sugar cane, a thick, fibrous plant, into the sweet granules Europeans demanded for their tea and cakes and candy. The owners organized their slaves into teams known as gangs. Gangs worked in the field, planting the cane or cutting it with a sugar knife; in the mill, where they pushed the cane between heavy rollers to squeeze out the juice; or in the boiling or curing house, where the juice was converted into crystals or molasses.

A horrifying description of the risks they faced comes from the journal of John Gabriel Stedman, a Dutch soldier who was stationed in Surinam, on the northeast coast of South America.

> So very dangerous is the work of those Negroes who enter the canes in the rollers, that should one of their fingers catch between them, which frequently happens by inadvertency, the whole arm is instantly shattered to atoms, if not part of the body, for which reason a hatchet is generally kept ready to chop off the limb, before the

as fast as we could, and went back to our employment till dark at night. We then shoveled up the salt in large heaps, and went down to the sea, where we washed the pickle from our limbs, and cleaned the barrows and shovels from the salt. When we returned to the house, our master gave us each our allowance of raw Indian corn, which we pounded in a mortar and boiled in water for our suppers.

Eventually Prince was sold to an owner who took her to England in 1828. She managed to escape, and her life story was the first account of a female slave to be published in Britain.

In this 1835 illustration, a Brazilian slave owner hits his female slave across the palm of her hand with a stick, as punishment for some error or misdeed.

working of the mill can be stopped. The other danger is that should a Negro slave dare to taste that sugar which he produces by the sweat of his brow, he would run the hazard of paying the expense by some hundred lashes, if not by the breaking out of all his teeth. Such are the hardships, and dangers, to which the sugar-making Negroes are exposed.

Although hardships abounded at the sugar mills, one task was more hated than most. A Scottish observer in the British island of St. Kitts wrote about the process of carrying manure from dung hills to fertilize the cane fields. The dung hills were mounds with "ashes from the boiling kettle, the bruised canes, the spilt leaves of the cane, the cleaning of the houses, and dung of the stables. . . ."

Every ten Negroes have a driver, who walks behind them, carrying in his hand a short whip and a long one . . . each has a little basket, which he carries up the hill filled with the manure and returns with a load of canes to the Mill. They go up at a trot, and return at a gallop, and did you not know the cruel necessity of this alertness, you would believe them the merriest people in the world.

As disgusting as the task sounds, it was also backbreaking. The "little basket" – which must have reeked and dripped in the heat of the day – weighed around seventy-five pounds (34 kilos).

Children as young as three were old enough to work, according to Thomas Roughley, the author of *The Jamaica Planter's Guide*. He recommended that plantation managers put toddlers under the care of an "old woman" in a "little playful gang." He said each slave child "should have a little basket, and be made somewhat useful by gathering up fallen trash and leaves, and pulling up young weeds."

Young or old, plantation slaves got small thanks for all their toil. Many of them were allowed a tiny plot of land where they could grow vegetables or even chickens or pigs, which they could sell. But the slaves had to manage these plots on their own scant time, usually on the one day a week they did not have to work. In Martinique, Pierre Dessalles gave his slaves an extra half day off to work their plots, not from the goodness of his heart, but because he sometimes couldn't afford to feed them.

Slaves in the Mines

The discovery of gold in Brazil in 1693 and diamonds in the 1720s created a demand for slaves to pan for gold or diamonds in the rivers, or dig for gold in hillside tunnels. Many slaves who were shipped to Brazil had worked in mines on the west coast of Africa, and knew more about the job than their owners did.

Mining is dangerous, even today. In those days there were no safety laws, and slaves were at constant risk of death from cave-ins and other accidents. And the cold, wet, and stony mines, where the slaves not only worked but also ate and slept, sapped their health. Pneumonia and other illnesses claimed many lives. One missionary said that owners did not expect their slave miners to survive more than seven years.

Some mine owners lived far from their slaves, and trusted them to give the owners a specified amount of gold and keep the rest to buy food. By 1784, many slaves had saved enough money to buy freedom for themselves and their children. Thousands of people won their freedom this way, and the Portuguese government became suspicious. How could so many slaves have saved up the price of freedom? The slaves were suspected of smuggling gold and diamonds out of the mines. Officials tried to catch them in the act, and imposed strict penalties on anyone who was caught, but people were so desperate for freedom that they were willing to take the risk.

Miners were not the only ones to buy their freedom in Brazil. Many owners, particularly in cities, rented their workers out as laborers and let them keep any money they earned above a certain amount. If they saved enough over time, they could become free.

Slaves under the Law

Everywhere in South America and the Caribbean, a slave was defined as anyone who had been bought or had been born to a slave mother. Martinique and other French colonies followed the Code Noir (Black Code) of 1685, which gave their slaves more protection than they had in other colonies. The law considered the slaves chattels – possessions – but recognized them as human beings with souls. All slaves in French islands had to be baptized as Catholics, and they could marry, though only if their masters let them. They were not supposed to work on Sundays or holidays, and masters had to take care of any who were

HUNGRY AS A SLAVE

Because the fertile land of the West Indies was devoted almost exclusively to sugar cane, there wasn't much room for other food crops. As a result, many of the slaves did not eat enough protein and vegetables and developed diseases such as rickets and scurvy. Male Caribbean slaves were, on average, three inches (almost 8 cm) shorter than those in the American South. The women were so badly fed that half of them never produced babies. So while the American slave population went up, the slave population of the British West Indies declined.

elderly or ill. Owners could not sell a husband, wife, and young children away from one another.

The Code Noir decreed that slaves could be beaten with rods or straps but could not be tortured or have a limb mutilated. It set out specific penalties for fugitive slaves absent for a month or more. After a first attempt, they would have their ears cut off and one shoulder branded with a fleur-de-lis, the symbol of France. A second try at running away would be punished by branding of the other shoulder and cutting of the slave's hamstring (the tendon at the back of the knee) to keep the slave from running anywhere at all. Any slave who tried to escape again would be killed.

In the British islands slaves could not marry, and there was no mention of baptism or religious education. The law described them as having a "wild, barbarous and savage nature, to be controlled only with strict severity," but it did recognize the need to guard them from "the cruelties and insolence of themselves, and other ill-tempered people or owners," and required their owners to feed, shelter, and clothe them. The law provided punishments for slaves who traded in stolen goods, hit Christians, or burned sugar cane. The penalty for stealing property or threatening or striking a white person was death. Runaway slaves were whipped; whites who gave them shelter could be fined, but blacks could be put to death.

In the Dutch islands, masters were officially prohibited from mutilating or killing their slaves, but sometimes even that seems to have been allowed. Stedman, the soldier, described a white woman who often abused her slaves. He said she drowned the infant of one slave in a stream because she could not tolerate the child's crying, and then flogged the mother when she tried to follow the baby to her death. One day some slaves begged her to be gentler, but that only enraged her more. She immediately had two slaves decapitated. The surviving slaves visited the governor of the colony and said:

> This, your Excellency, is the head of my son, and this is the head of my brother, struck off by our mistress's command for endeavoring to prevent murder. We know our evidence is nothing in a state of slavery, but if these bloody heads etc. are sufficient proof of what we say, we only beg that such may be prevented in time to come, when we will all cheerfully spill our blood and our sweat for the preservation and prosperity of our master and mistress.

In 1833, the British government introduced the treadmill in prisons as a more "humane" punishment than floggings. The treadmill consisted of rows of wooden steps around a hollow cylinder. Slave owners in the Caribbean also found this a useful tool. Guards with whips kept the slaves moving quickly from step to step. If they fainted or stopped from exhaustion, the steps would hit them.

A slave's word was never trusted over an owner's. If a white person had seen the carnage, Stedman said, the woman would have been punished, though only with a fifty-pound fine for each murder. But no white person had witnessed her vicious behavior, so the slaves were flogged for telling a lie.

Slave Religion

Owners were always afraid that slaves would rise up against them, so they tried to control what slaves were allowed to think, as well as what they were allowed to do. Laws were passed to wipe out any traces of African religion, languages, and customs. For example, beating drums, blowing horns, and using other loud instruments were banned. The Code Noir prohibited slaves who belonged to different masters from gathering, for fear that they might be plotting rebellion.

Nevertheless, slaves practiced their African rituals and faiths, even though they had to do so in secret. Although their religions varied greatly, many included worship of ancestors and gods, and made use of herbs and charms. In their new homes, they adapted such customs to suit their new needs. For example, Voodoo came to Haiti from Dahomey in Africa. One of its deities is from Africa and is considered tranquil and generous, while another, originating in America, is considered angry and impatient – which truly reflected the slaves' experiences in the New World.

In the practice of Obeah, sorcerers known as Obeah men used charms and herbs to heal, or to punish one slave at the request of another. Obeah made the rulers of the British colony of Jamaica so uneasy that they investigated whether Obeah men really could cause death or injury. In a report in 1789, they wrote that Africans go to them "with the most implicit faith, upon all occasions, whether for the cure of disorders, the obtaining of revenge for injuries or insults, the conciliating of favor, the discovery and punishment of the thief or the adulterer, and the predicting of future events." The British banned Obeah.

Even those slaves who converted to Christianity often mixed parts of their old faiths with the new. They were trying, as much as they could, to hang onto some traces of the lives they had known in Africa, in this new and difficult world.

Escape to Freedom

Sometimes plantation owners freed their slaves in their wills, and in Brazil, Cuba, and Puerto Rico, slaves could buy their freedom. In other places, freedom couldn't be bought but an owner might decide to free a slave – usually if the slave was old, or was his own child. But most slaves could only become free by running away.

Newspapers often announced rewards for runaway slaves. One from the Kingston, Jamaica, *Daily Advertiser*, on January 29, 1790, said:

RAN AWAY
From her owners, about the month of Sept. last, a short creole wench named
DILIGENCE, alias JUNK
has a large scar on her breast, occasioned by a burn, with a toe off each foot, for
which she wears slippers. Speaks very slow and artful.

In the early seventeenth century, Brazilian soldiers were offered gold as a reward for finding runaways. Sometimes they returned with innocent slaves who had simply been on an errand for their owners. Captured runaways were branded with the letter *F* to show that they were fugitives, but that didn't stop them. Some tried a second time, risking the loss of an ear if they were found, and even a third time, though the punishment would be death.

The artist who drew this elderly spiritual healer had watched her at work, and left us a description of the way she used her powers in an effort to cure someone of an illness. Such healers were often old women called Mama Snekie, or Mama of Snakes.

Slaves who had a trade and managed to escape to cities stood a chance of blending in, but most runaways looked for safe haven in the forests and swamplands, where other escapees had started colonies called *quilombos*. One *quilombo*, Palmares, survived for seventy years in northeastern Brazil. At first the residents raided nearby villages for food, but eventually they became self-sufficient and created a vibrant community where as many as twenty thousand people lived. Most of them were from what is today Angola, on Africa's southwest coast, and they brought their Angolan way of life to Palmares. They lived in several settlements surrounded by a larger village, and were ruled by a king. Palmares lasted until 1695, when the Portuguese conquered it with an army of seven thousand soldiers.

In the Dutch colony of Surinam most plantations were along rivers bordered by swampland or forests. Slaves easily escaped into the interior of the country, where few whites lived. Some plantations lost their entire workforce. The runaways were known as maroons, from the Spanish word *cimarrón*, meaning "wild."

The owners asked the Netherlands for volunteers to help the local troops capture deserters, but still the maroons could not be conquered. Eventually the

A CELEBRATED SLAVE

Slaves did not receive any education, but the medical discovery of one slave in Surinam lives on in its botanical name, *Quassia amara*. Physicians there couldn't find a cure for high fevers that were ravaging the population, but in 1730 the slave Quassie Graman discovered a remedy using the bark of a local tree. The masters were so impressed with his cure that they asked for his help. Quassie told his secret cure to a plantation owner who was interested in botany (the study of plants). That owner told the secret to a noted Swedish botanist, Carl Linnaeus, who named the tree after the slave. This discovery is not Quassie's only claim to fame. He was also renowned as a healer and a maker and seller of magical amulets.

Graman Quassie visited John Gabriel Stedman, a Dutch soldier stationed in Surinam, wearing the gold-laced coat and gold medal that he had received from William V, Prince of Orange. Quassie had helped in the fight against bands of runaway slaves. In recognition of his services, Surinam's colonial governor had sent him to the Netherlands to meet the Dutch ruler.

government negotiated agreements with them. In Jamaica, in 1739, the government gave the maroon leader Cudjoe rights to the west of the island, in exchange for the maroons' help in ending local slave revolts.

The sad fact, however, is that most slaves died in captivity. Freedom would not come until slavery was ended in South America and the Caribbean. For millions, that would be too late.

CHAPTER 8
"THE MONSTER IS DEAD!": BRITISH ABOLITION

Granville Sharp, 1820

Late one afternoon in 1765, a line of people waited outside the office of William Sharp in London. Dr. Sharp was known for offering medical care to people who couldn't afford to pay for it. One of the men in line stood out; his face was bloody, beaten beyond recognition, and his skin was black. Black people were not totally unknown in London – there were several thousand of them – but they were not common, either.

The young man's name was Jonathan Strong, and his story was a pitiful one. He was a slave from Barbados, living in London with his owner, David Lisle. Lisle beat Strong so hard and so often that he walked with a limp. But this time, Lisle had become so furious with Strong that he had pistol-whipped him until his gun had broken. Thinking he had beaten his slave to the point of uselessness, Lisle had then abandoned him. Fortunately, someone had directed the young man to the doctor's clinic.

William Sharp's brother Granville happened to step out of the office and see Strong. Both Sharp brothers would become saviors to the young man, in different ways. For the moment, Strong needed medical care, which would require more than four months in the hospital. He had suffered permanent eye damage, but he was healthy enough for the brothers to find him a job with a nearby pharmacist, a Mr. Brown. Now he was an employee – no longer anyone's slave.

Two years later, Lisle spotted Strong working as a footman for the pharmacist's wife. A slave – even one whom Lisle had no use for – was worth money, and Strong was a lot healthier than when Lisle had left him for dead. So he had Strong picked up by the Lord Mayor's officers and thrown into prison. Lisle planned to keep him there until he could be sold to a sea captain and shipped off to one of Britain's colonies in the Americas.

Strong, who had learned to read and write during his two years of freedom, immediately sent notes to people who might help him, including Granville Sharp. When Sharp arrived in the gloom of the prison, he was enraged. The authorities had no right to hold the young man, who had done nothing wrong, he said. Moreover, Strong had the right to a hearing by the Lord Mayor. And indeed the

Lord Mayor agreed that "the lad had not stolen anything and was not guilty of any offence and was therefore at liberty to go away."

As word spread among London's Africans that a man named Granville Sharp had helped free a slave, more of them came to see him. In 1768, he secured a court order to ship a woman slave back from the West Indies to Britain on the grounds that she had been illegally deported. In 1770, he helped free another kidnapped African before he could be shipped off to Jamaica.

Then came the case of James Somerset – a trial that changed history. Somerset visited Sharp the morning of January 13, 1772. He'd arrived in England with his owner, had escaped and been recaptured, and had then been released by a court order until his appeal could be heard by Lord Chief Justice Mansfield. This was just the case Sharp was looking for. Way back in the 1500s, a court had decreed that the moment slaves "put their foot on English ground, that moment they became free." Yet there were thousands of black slaves in England. Somerset's case would force the courts to answer this question once and for all: Was slavery legal on English soil?

Sharp prepared a twenty-eight-page pamphlet that he sent to Somerset's lawyers and the judges. At the hearings, which began in February 1772, one of Somerset's lawyers reminded the court of that long-ago decision. "In those days," he noted, "it was resolved that England was too pure an air for slaves to breathe in." But the lawyers for Somerset's owner predicted dire economic consequences if every black slave in England was set free.

The case lasted for months, and caught the public's fancy. People read long articles about it in the papers, and so many came to watch the proceedings that there were not enough seats to hold them all.

In the end, the Lord Chief Justice ruled in favor of James Somerset, saying that a master had no right to force a slave to go into a foreign country. Although his decision did not state that slavery was illegal in England, most people understood him to mean just that. And when, on June 22, 1772, Lord Mansfield ruled that "the Man must be discharged," the Africans watching from the court's public space bowed deeply to the justice and shook hands with each other.

Thomas Clarkson

The abolitionists in England, and later in the United States, were not people who had been slaves like Spartacus, fighting for their own freedom. They had nothing

Thomas Clarkson

QUAKERS MAKE THEMSELVES HEARD

Many of those who fought for abolition did so because of their personal religious beliefs, but in Britain and America the Religious Society of Friends, commonly known as Quakers, worked for abolition as a group. The religion is rooted in a belief that all people own an element of God's spirit, and all are therefore equal in God's eyes.

Shortly after George Fox started the religion in seventeenth-century England, he wrote to American Quakers who "have Blacks and Indian slaves,"

personal at stake. They were determined to abolish slavery simply because it was wrong. Granville Sharp had taken individual cases to court. Now someone was needed to organize a movement to abolish slavery. The person turned out to be Thomas Clarkson, who was studying to be an Anglican clergyman at the University of Cambridge. His interest in slavery began in 1785 when he entered an essay-writing contest with a paper, written in Latin, on the topic "Is it lawful to make slaves of others against their wills?"

He didn't enjoy working for the prize. How could he, he asked himself, when the work was colored by all the human suffering he had uncovered in his research: the violent capture of slaves, the separation of families, the miserable voyages across the Atlantic?

"It was one gloomy subject from morning to night," he wrote. "I no longer regarded my essay as a mere trial for literary distinction. My great desire was to produce a work that should call forth a vigorous public effort to redress the wrongs of injured Africa." Still, he threw himself into the subject, reading as much as he could get his hands on. He won the essay contest.

On the way home from reading his essay aloud at the award ceremony, he got off his horse and began to think, "if the contents of the Essay were true, it was time some person should see these calamities to their end."

Over the course of the next sixty years, Clarkson fought these calamities almost without letup. He logged 35,000 miles (56,000 km) of travel through Britain, mostly on horseback, gathering evidence, interviewing witnesses, setting up local committees, and speaking at meetings. He kept notes and diaries, published pamphlets calling attention to the mistreatment of slaves, and wrote letters to political figures and fellow activists. Sometimes he risked his health, even his life.

Clarkson soon made contact with the Quakers, and they published his *Essay on the Slavery and Commerce of the Human Species, particularly the African* in 1786. He also learned about Granville Sharp's activities, and met James Ramsay, an Anglican minister back from the West Indies who could describe slavery firsthand. The three men banded together with others, and on May 22, 1787, their group, the Society for Effecting the Abolition of the Slave Trade, held its first meeting.

With these three solid Anglicans on board, the new society had an aura of respectability. The members came to a practical compromise with their ideals. Although all of them hated slavery, they decided to first concentrate on convincing Parliament to abolish the slave *trade*, not slavery itself. They knew that two groups would fight them every step of the way: wealthy merchants in London, Liverpool, Bristol, and Manchester, whose businesses made huge profits on the slave trade, and Caribbean plantation owners, who got rich on the cotton, tobacco, rice, and indigo (blue dye) grown on their estates. Some of these merchants and landowners lived in Britain, and some even had seats in Parliament. It was simply not realistic to try to end slavery – not yet.

But the members had faith that eliminating the trade in human beings would be a first step toward abolishing slavery itself. If the fresh supply of Africans was cut off, slave owners would have to treat their slaves better to keep them healthy enough to work. Soon the owners would discover that it was more profitable to pay slaves for their labor than to keep them in bondage. Then, they believed, slavery would wither away.

To bring an end to the slave trade, Parliament would have to pass a law, and it might well be voted down. So Clarkson's next step was to find an ally to spearhead the campaign in Parliament. He was introduced to William Wilberforce, a Member of Parliament (MP) with a reputation as an eloquent speaker. Clarkson would supply him with the information he needed, and Wilberforce would make the case in Parliament. Clarkson would also find ways to swing public opinion behind the campaign. Although only one in ten British men (and no women) could vote in elections, MPs read the newspapers and were keenly aware of which issues were capturing the public imagination.

The Enemies of Abolition

With their organization in place, Clarkson set out to collect evidence about slavery and the slave trade. His investigations took him to ports where slave ships docked. The tall, red-headed Clarkson was easy to spot, and his opponents were quick to find him. He had many

reminding them that all people were equal. After a visit to Barbados he observed, "If you were in the same condition as the Blacks are . . . you would think it . . . very great Bondage and Cruelty." Over the next century, the Religious Society of Friends condemned slave trading; they disowned any Quaker who kept slaves, and finally, in 1772, they called publicly for total abolition.

The Quakers realized that most English people considered them to be oddballs. Among other things, they looked different; they wore simple clothes instead of the fancy silks and satins of the day, the women left their bonnets untrimmed, and the men refused to carry weapons. The Quakers knew they would have to reach sympathetic Anglicans, people the British public would take seriously. Anthony Benezet helped make this happen by writing pamphlets and letters that touched hearts in Europe. He had grown up in England and had become a Quaker in Pennsylvania. His pamphlet *Some Historical Account of Guinea*, published in 1771, tells of a recently arrived slave "who appeared thoughtful and dejected, frequently dropping tears when taking notice of his master's children." No one understood his sadness until the man learned English and could share his story: "He had a wife and children in his own country; . . . some of these being sick and thirsty, he went in the night time to fetch water at a spring, where he was violently seized and carried away by persons who lay in wait to catch men, from whence he was transported to America." Benezet was outraged. "When, and how, have these oppressed people forfeited their liberty? . . . Have they not the same right to demand it, as any of us should have, if we have been violently snatched by pirates from our native land?"

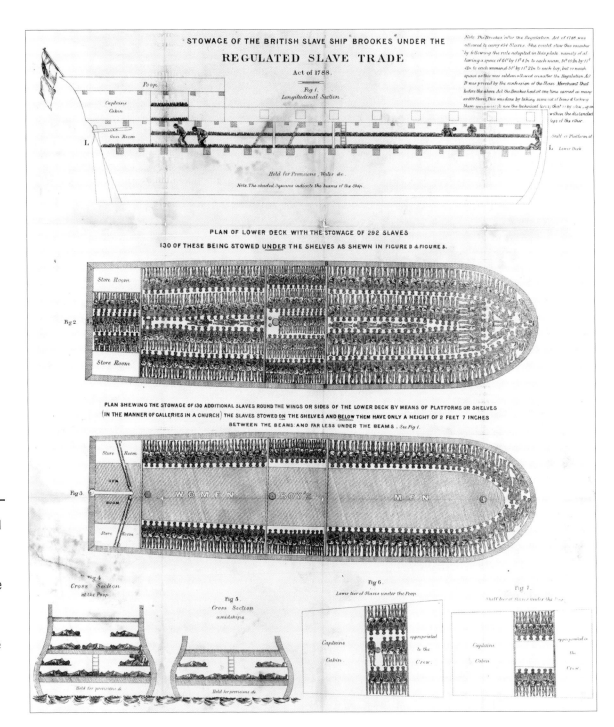

Antislavery campaigners used this shocking diagram of the slave ship *Brookes*, with 482 human beings stacked up like cargo, to inflame the public against the slave trade. The drawing appeared everywhere — in newspapers, books, pamphlets, even on the walls of taverns.

frightening encounters with them. Once, he had just started walking away from the end of a Liverpool pier when he noticed eight or nine people walking toward him:

> I expected that they would have divided to let me through them; instead of which they closed upon me. . . . [It suddenly struck me] that they had a design to throw me over the pier head. Vigorous on account of the danger, I darted forward. One of them against whom I pushed myself, fell down. Their ranks were broken and I escaped not without blows amidst their imprecations and abuse.

That he had opponents was not surprising. Almost everywhere he traveled, people's livelihood could be traced, directly or indirectly, to slavery. Warehouses in Bristol were teeming with West Indian goods – tobacco, cocoa, and sugar, which was refined in Bristol. As for Liverpool, more than 300,000 slaves were shipped from there between 1783 and 1793, many of the slave ships were built there, and the salaries of many laborers, from sailmakers to barrel makers, depended on this trade. Clarkson received threatening letters telling him to leave the city on his own, or he would not leave alive. But he was a brave man, and he stayed.

He boarded ships to measure the slaves' quarters. He tried to speak to captains or crew members, but most of them avoided him for fear of losing their jobs. He had more luck with the surgeons who worked on board the overcrowded ships. These doctors treated the diseases that sickened or killed so many, and helped the captains select healthy slaves for purchase in Africa. Two surgeons, James Arnold and Alexander Falconbridge, were uneasy about this work. Arnold had taken the job because he was in debt, and planned to go on only one more voyage. He agreed to keep notes for Clarkson. Falconbridge, who had gone on four trips, had quit because he was sickened by the human suffering he had witnessed. He assured Clarkson he'd be willing to testify before a parliamentary committee about what he'd seen. A member of Clarkson's society compiled Falconbridge's observations into a booklet published in February 1788. Now the public could read about the Middle Passage:

> The place allotted for the sick Negroes is under the half deck, where they lie on the bare planks. By this means, those who are emaciated, frequently have their skin, and

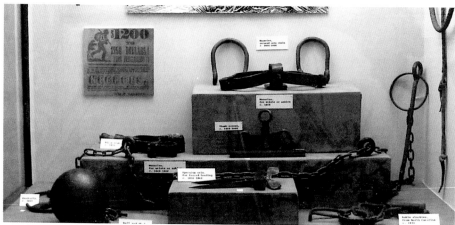

Handcuffs and leg shackles such as these infuriated Thomas Clarkson, as did thumbscrews — used to torture slaves by squeezing their thumbs — and a device for prying open the mouth of any slave attempting suicide by refusing food. When he saw these objects for sale in a naval supply shop in Liverpool, the abolitionist purchased them to expose the cruel practices of slave traders.

Josiah Wedgwood, a brilliant English potter, was an early supporter of the campaign to end the slave trade. His company designed this logo of a chained slave with the slogan "Am I Not a Man and a Brother?" Abolitionists had the logo printed on leaflets or cast into medallions for people to wear.

even their flesh, entirely rubbed off, by the motion of the ship, from the prominent parts of the shoulders, elbows, and hips, so as to render the bones in those parts quite bare. . . . The surgeon, upon going between decks, in the morning, . . . frequently finds several dead.

Africans were not the only unwilling passengers on the slave ships. British men were often tricked into signing on as sailors and then cheated out of their pay. On board, they were often brutalized. One sailor had hot pitch (tar) poured on his back, another was chained to the deck for days, and floggings were common. Some caught tropical diseases like malaria and yellow fever. Inspecting the records of the Customs House in London, Clarkson discovered that, on average, only eight out of every ten white sailors survived a voyage on the Middle Passage. This would be useful information; people might care more about slave trading if they knew how many white Englishmen were among the victims.

The Campaign Begins

On his way back to London, Clarkson stopped in Manchester, a booming industrial city whose factories manufactured cloth from slave-grown cotton. He expected to meet hostility there, but to his surprise a group of citizens was already hatching a plan to petition Parliament against the slave trade; they invited him to preach on Sunday. He chose as his theme the biblical words "Thou shalt not oppress a stranger: for ye know the heart of a stranger, seeing ye were strangers in the land of Egypt," and was moved to see "a great crowd of black people standing round the pulpit." Sometime after his visit, Manchester's antislavery committee sent a petition to Parliament with the signatures of more than ten thousand people, one-fifth of the city's population.

Clarkson returned to London armed with facts, figures, displays, and the names of eyewitnesses willing to testify. The society sent out newsletters and asked for donations, all to arouse public sentiment. Soon, the slave trade question seemed to be on everyone's lips. Public debates were popular entertainment at that time, and in February alone London saw seven on the question of abolition of the slave trade.

Women's Voices

Women were not allowed to vote or to hold public office, but they had opinions; many were appalled by slavery and carried the antislavery message into their own parlors and dining rooms. Since West Indian sugar was tainted by the suffering of the African slaves who produced it, they decided that they would simply refuse to buy it.

A poem by Mary Birkett, a young Quaker, told women they had a choice: use sugar and continue to harm slaves, or reject the "bloodstained luxury" to help them gain their freedom:

If we no more the blood-stained lux'ry choose . . .
Say not that small's the sphere in which we move, . . .
Not so – we hold a most important share,
In all the evils – all the wrongs they bear.

The anti-sugar campaign caught on. As Clarkson traveled around Britain, he kept track of how many people were boycotting sugar and estimated that "no fewer than three hundred thousand persons had abandoned the use of sugar."

This poster advertised sugar bowls with the words "East India Sugar not made by Slaves," so that people could assure their guests that the sugar they were putting in their tea had been produced by free laborers in the East Indies, not West Indian slaves.

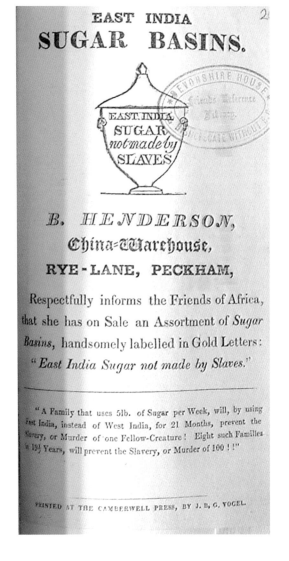

BLACK ACTIVISTS

Although many former slaves were living in London, Clarkson never invited any of them to speak at parliamentary hearings. Why? Even the most humane abolitionists of that time gave more weight to the observations of whites than to the actual experiences of blacks. Yet many blacks did influence public opinion through their writings.

PHILLIS WHEATLEY

Phillis Wheatley was kidnapped from Africa when she was only eight, and bought by John Wheatley, a merchant and tailor in Boston. The Wheatleys treated her like a member of the family and taught her to read the Bible. She taught herself to write. Soon she was composing poetry, and in 1773 she visited England, where her book, *Poems on Various Subjects, Religious and Moral*, was published. It created quite a sensation, since many English people doubted that an African could develop her mind as a white person could. After the publication of her poems, her master freed her, and she became a speaker at public antislavery meetings. Her poem on being kidnapped by slave traders was published in 1789, as the abolition movement caught fire in Britain:

Phillis Wheatley's popular poems were not only about slavery. She wrote verses of comfort over the death of a child, and even addressed a poem of praise to the British king.

I, young in life, by seeming cruel fate,
Was snach'd from Afric's fancy'd happy seat;
What pangs excruciating must molest,
What sorrows labour in my parents' breast?

OTTOBAH CUGOANO

Ottobah Cugoano became a slave when he was kidnapped in Africa and sold for a gun, a piece of cloth, and some lead. His book, *Thoughts and Sentiments on the Evil and wicked Traffic of the Human Species*, published in 1787, details the heartless treatment of slaves in Grenada, where "for eating a piece of sugar-cane, some were cruelly lashed, or struck over the face, to knock their teeth out." Cugoano asks his readers why the British, "who ought to be considered as the most learned and civilized people in the world . . . should carry on a traffic of the most barbarous cruelty and injustice, and [why] many think slavery, robbery and murder no crime?" He even insists that slaves have as much of a duty to escape and resist as anyone who is robbed, since "the enslaver is a robber."

OLAUDAH EQUIANO

Olaudah Equiano was first a slave to a British naval officer, who named him Gustavus Vassa and took him on many sea voyages; then to a sea captain, who took him to the West Indies; and finally to a Quaker merchant from Philadelphia, who let him buy his freedom for forty pounds when he was about twenty years old. His book, *The Interesting Narrative of the Life of Olaudah Equiano, or Gustavus Vassa*, which he published in 1789, was a potent weapon in the fight against slavery. It chronicles the horrors of slavery that Equiano observed firsthand.

It was Equiano who told Granville Sharp about the captain of the *Zong*, who threw 133 living slaves off his ship to cash in on the insurance money.

GUSTAVUS VASSA.

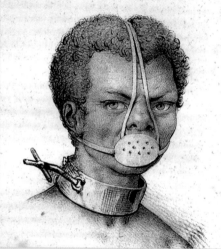

Olaudah Equiano's *Interesting Narrative* describes "a black woman slave... cruelly loaded with various kinds of iron machines; she had one particularly on her head, which locked her mouth so fast she could scarcely speak; and could not eat nor drink."

Women rarely gave public speeches in the late 1700s, but the slavery issue began to draw them out. Some appeared in antislavery debates. Others used their pens to attack slavery. Famous playwright and poet Hannah More wrote "Slavery, a Poem" to evoke the horrors of an African slave raid, from the "burning village and the blazing town" to the separation of a "shrieking babe" from its mother.

Slow Progress in Parliament

Pamphlets, books, poems, the sugar boycott, and petitions to Parliament – 102 in 1788 alone – were preparing the ground for the parliamentary vote. But in Parliament, things moved slowly. In 1789, a year after debate on the slave trade had begun, Wilberforce's bill against the trade was defeated by a vote of 163 to 88. His opponents said that a British law wouldn't end the slave trade at all; it would only let the French pick up the business dropped by the British, and make them rich.

The abolitionists did not give up. Wilberforce continued to introduce bills against the slave trade. If one passed in both sections of Parliament – the House of Commons and the House of Lords – it would become law. In 1792, one of his bills garnered a huge majority in the House of Commons – 230 votes to 85 – but it was rejected by the House of Lords.

At that point, just as abolition began to seem within reach, disaster struck.

Terror Takes Over

On July 14, 1789, French revolutionaries stormed the Bastille, a prison in Paris, igniting a bloody ten-year revolution that would take the lives of many upper-class people, including the king and queen. The revolutionaries' cry for "Liberty, Equality, Fraternity" rang far beyond France's borders. As word of the revolution began to reach St-Domingue (today's Haiti), a Caribbean island where half a million Africans toiled in French sugar plantations and mills under some of the worst conditions in the New World, the slaves began to hope that the revolution would bring them freedom as well. But the new French government was not ready to extend liberty *that* far; the sugar plantations produced too much wealth for France.

The government's refusal to free the slaves prompted the largest and most violent slave revolt in the Americas. In 1791 the slaves burned cane fields, sugar mills, and their masters' estates; they wrecked machinery; and with their machetes they

The French complained that Toussaint L'Ouverture's troops were everywhere. As one soldier said, "Each tree, each hole, each piece of rock hid from our unseeing eyes a cowardly assassin." But William Wordsworth, the famous English poet, celebrated Toussaint's triumphs: "Live and take comfort. Thou hast left behind / Powers that will work for thee; air, earth, and skies. . . ."

slaughtered white men, women, and children. So terrified were the whites of St-Domingue that ten thousand fled to the United States.

Toussaint L'Ouverture is sometimes called the "Black Spartacus" for his part in the revolt. He didn't begin the rebellion, and he wasn't even a slave anymore. In fact, he himself was a slave owner who managed an estate worked by slaves. At first he tried to protect his owner's property, but after his owner escaped to safety, Toussaint joined the revolt against the French.

Spain and Britain were trying to take advantage of France's weakness to capture the colony for its riches. For Toussaint, this was the way to end slavery: the rebels would side with France's enemies. Even the French praised his brilliant tactics. The French were defeated and St-Domingue's slaves were freed in 1794.

Toussaint switched sides again, back to the French this time. They realized that he was a popular leader who commanded respect so they appointed him governor general. With a third of the slave population dead and hundreds of plantations destroyed, Toussaint knew he had to revive the sugar industry. He made an unpopular decision: he would not drive out the old plantation owners, or divide the plantations into smaller plots for the people; he was afraid they would not produce enough wealth for the island. Instead, he forced former slaves to work for their old masters, though he reduced the working hours and forbade owners to whip their workers. Although he succeeded in restoring two-thirds of the plantations to production, the ex-slaves were upset. After all the bloodshed, why did they still have to live on white-owned plantations?

Meanwhile, the French decided to launch a new invasion of Haiti, secretly planning to take over the government from Toussaint and reintroduce slavery. With his popularity weakened, they found it easy to kidnap Toussaint and throw him into a French prison, where he died of ill treatment in a cold, damp cell. In the end, though, the French could not win against yellow fever and the Haitian people. Having lost sixty thousand soldiers and sailors, they left the island, and Haiti proclaimed its independence in 1804.

In Britain there was fear that slave revolts would spread throughout the other islands in the Caribbean, and they did: to Grenada, St. Vincent, St. Lucia, and Jamaica. Here was an argument that the slave owners and slave traders could use against the abolitionists: Show our slaves any weakness, and they will turn on us.

But the cry of "Liberty, Equality, Fraternity" was heard in Britain too. Organizations of radical workers popped up, and as reports began to arrive of the murder of two thousand French aristocrats in September 1792, Britain's ruling classes were gripped by fear. Would they too be stripped of wealth and power, perhaps even murdered?

In February 1794, the French revolutionary government abolished slavery in all its colonies, making France the first European country to do so. In Britain some people blamed the hated French for abolitionist ideas, while others blamed British abolitionists for the slave revolt in St-Domingue. Thomas Clarkson, who made no secret of his sympathies for the French Revolution, was accused of being a dangerous radical. Mobs burned radicals' books and even their homes. The government passed two bills against speech that might "excite or stir up the people to hatred or contempt of the . . . constitution of this realm" and required a magistrate's approval for any public meeting of more than fifty people. Though Wilberforce continued to introduce his bills year after year, from 1794 through 1799, the time was not ripe for abolitionism.

Abolitionism Revived

It was not until 1804 that the abolition movement regained its momentum. France's leader, Napoleon, had declared himself emperor, and had reintroduced slavery. Since the British detested Napoleon – he had threatened to invade Britain – it was now acceptable for them to oppose slavery.

Once again, pamphlets were published, women boycotted sugar, and Wilberforce took up the cause in Parliament. Abolitionist committees were revived. Support in the House of Commons was growing as well. Finally, in January 1806, Parliament renewed its debate on abolishing slavery.

This time the atmosphere was different. St-Domingue had defeated the French and become independent, so no one could argue that the French would pick up the slave trade once the British pulled out. And now eyewitness reports on slavery were heard by the full House of Commons, not just by committees. Sir John Doyle, a former officer in the West Indies, told the House of hearing terrible groans coming from a hut. When he and his troops stepped inside, they found a slave chained and "stretched upon the ground, where for four days he had remained without being able to change his position. . . . The rats had actually eaten off the greater part of both his ears." In February 1807, this bill passed: "That this House, conceiving the African Slave Trade to be contrary to the principles of justice, humanity, and sound policy, will, with all practicable expedition, proceed to take effectual measures for abolishing the said trade."

Like many abolitionists, Clarkson believed that they had done God's work by ending the slave trade. The next day he wrote to a friend,

I want words to express the joy I feel on the occasion. In favour of the Motion there were 203. Against it 16. . . . I shall leave London with a heart full of gratitude to the Parent of all mercies [God], that he has been pleased thus far to render a portion of my life useful to my oppressed fellow creatures.

Making Freedom a Reality

Meanwhile, slaves were still hoeing the sugar-cane fields of Barbados and crushing cane in the mills of Jamaica. As the supply of fresh slaves dried up with the end of the slave trade, some planters began to feed their slaves better food, and even installed safety devices to protect them against accidents. Still, slavery did not wither away as the abolitionists had hoped.

In 1823, veteran activists from the old antislavery society, together with some help, formed the London Society for Mitigating and Gradually Abolishing the State of Slavery Throughout the British Dominions. They thought the country would not accept more rapid change. Once again Clarkson hit the road, covering ten thousand miles (16,000 km) twice within a year, and organizing 230 branches that presented 777 petitions to Parliament. This time, the public was one step ahead of the committee. As Clarkson wrote, "Everywhere People are asking me about *immediate abolition*."

Women's Voices Again

Now women took the lead. Elizabeth Heyrick was one of them. The title of her pamphlet was clear and straightforward: *Immediate, not Gradual Abolition*. Heyrick was a Quaker schoolteacher who believed that "truth and justice make their best way in the world when they appear in bold and simple majesty." She saw no reason for delay.

With characteristic directness, she urged grocers to refuse to stock slave-grown products, comparing this to receiving stolen goods from a thief. In the 1826 parliamentary elections, she encouraged people to vote only for candidates who supported immediate abolition.

Women organized their own antislavery clubs. In Sheffield, where the men's antislavery society was urging gradualism, the women's clubs called for immediate abolition. Today's politicians and activists often go door to door to promote their ideas; it was female abolitionists in Birmingham who introduced the practice. They knocked on doors to present their ideas to 80 percent of the households in that city. One man, an antislavery activist himself, marveled at their efficiency:

> Ladies Associations . . . did everything. They circulated publications: they procured the money to publish; they dunned & talked & coaxed & lectured: they got up public meetings & filled our halls & platforms when the day arrived; they carried round petitions & enforced the duty of signing them. . . . In a word they formed the cement of the whole Antislavery building – without their aid we never should have kept standing.

Slave Revolts

The abolitionists' voices carried throughout England and beyond, to the Caribbean islands, where slaves were heard singing:

> Oh me good friend Mr. Wilberforce mek me free
> God Almighty thank ye! God Almighty thank ye!
> God Almighty mek me free!

Those slaves who worked in the ports met sailors who shared the news from overseas, and those who served their masters and mistresses heard talk at the dinner tables. What they learned about Wilberforce and the abolitionists gave them hope, and sometimes spurred them into action.

In the port city of Georgetown in Demerara (now Guyana), rumors spread among the slaves that the king had already freed them. Led by black deacons of the church of young John Smith, a sympathetic white Protestant missionary who was secretly teaching slave children to read, the slaves demanded to speak

A SINGULAR EVENT IN HISTORY

Why did the abolition movement begin in Britain, and why did it succeed?

Historians are not sure, but they point out that abolition movements happened only in Western cultures — in Britain, the United States, and Europe. Asia, Africa, and the Middle East have never produced mass movements to end slavery.

Two forces in the West encouraged people to question slavery.

The first was religion. Western civilization is rooted in the Jewish and Christian Bibles. Although many slave owners found words in the Bible that seemed to allow slavery, the abolitionists focused on the Bible's story of a God who sides with slaves against their oppressors.

The second was an eighteenth-century movement called the Enlightenment. Philosophers like John Locke in England and Montesquieu in France taught an idea that was radical for their time: all people are born free and equal and share the same basic human rights. Abolitionists were influenced by this view, and used it to fight anyone who believed that a person could own another human being.

with the governor. They told him that "God had made them of the same flesh and blood as the whites, and that they were tired of being Slaves to them, that their good King had sent orders they should be free and they would not work anymore."

What began with words ended in bloodshed. Thousands of slaves revolted. By the time the uprising was quashed, government troops had killed 250 slaves and imprisoned Smith on charges of inciting the rebellion, which he almost certainly did not do. From his damp prison cell he smuggled out these verses from the Bible: "We are troubled on every side, yet not distressed; we are perplexed, but not in despair; persecuted, but not forsaken; cast down, but not destroyed." He had been sentenced to be hanged. Authorities in London relented, but by the time word of reprieve reached Demerara it was too late — he had died of tuberculosis. His story was covered widely in the British press, and public sympathy for him increased the support for ending slavery.

In Jamaica, as in Demerara, the slaves' hopes rose when they heard rumors that the king had freed them. When Christmas 1831 fell on a Sunday and the planters refused them an extra day off work, the slaves were furious. Samuel Sharpe, a slave preacher, traveled the island to organize resistance against the planters, who he said were standing in the way of their freedom. He was most likely trying to organize a strike for paid labor, but the result was a rebellion that involved between twenty thousand and thirty thousand slaves. The white death toll was remarkably low — only fourteen men — but more than two hundred plantations were torched. The government responded swiftly and harshly. Two hundred rebels were killed and more than three hundred were executed later, including Samuel Sharpe.

Said an eyewitness to Sharpe's hanging, "He marched to the spot . . . with a firm and even dignified step, clothed in a suit of new white clothes, made for him by some female members of the family of his owner, with all of whom he was a favorite, and who deeply regretted his untimely end." To this day, Jamaicans remember his last words: "I would rather die upon yonder gallows than live in slavery."

Jamaican colonists blamed missionaries for the rebellion, and churchmen had to flee in fear to Britain. There, their stories of white brutality toward slaves turned public opinion further against slavery and its supporters. British officials predicted more uprisings. As a vice admiral explained to a parliamentary committee, "The only reason why [the slaves] are tranquil now is, that they . . . hope to be emancipated." If they were not, he warned, "insurrection will soon take place."

"The Monster Is Dead!"

By 1830 there were 1,200 local antislavery groups in Britain, demanding immediate emancipation of slaves. But Parliament was still run by the rich and titled, many of whom got their wealth through slave labor. Only a small percentage of Englishmen were allowed to vote; a city as large and rich (and pro-abolition) as Manchester had no MPs at all. A bill that would allow more Englishmen to vote was introduced in 1831, but the House of Lords voted it down. The public became angrier, and it began to dawn on the government that they could face a rebellion if they did not pass a reform bill soon. They did so in 1832, and many antislavery members were elected.

In 1833 the new Parliament met, and the antislavery forces led an orderly demonstration down to the prime minister's office on Downing Street. Finally, in the summer of 1833, an emancipation bill passed both houses.

It did not free the slaves immediately. Instead, emancipation would come in two stages. First, slaves would become "apprentices," doing full-time unpaid work for their owners for six years. Only then would they be free. This was not popular among the antislavery activists, and one extraordinary petition against the delay arrived in Parliament with the signatures of more than half a million women. In the West Indies, slaves went on strike. Finally the "apprenticeship" period was shortened to four years. On August 1, 1838, almost 800,000 slaves throughout the British Caribbean were freed.

In one Jamaican church, on the night before, the slaves held a ceremony. They had hung the walls with garlands of flowers and portraits of Thomas Clarkson and William Wilberforce. In the churchyard was a coffin labeled "Colonial Slavery, died July 31st, 1838, aged 276 years." In the coffin they placed an iron punishment collar, a whip, and chains.

At midnight, their minister cried, "The monster is dead!"

And so it was – in the British West Indies.

CHAPTER 9
IN THE LAND OF LIBERTY: NORTH AMERICA

One July 4 in the early 1800s, cannon blasts woke Charles Ball in Columbia, South Carolina. Fifes and drums played all morning, and at noon several hundred people sat down at a long table to eat, drink, and sing songs in honor of liberty. It was America's Independence Day.

All day Ball heard speakers praise the nation. One speaker said that it was a "principle of our free government that all men were born free and equal." But Ball knew the words did not apply to him. He was a slave and on this Independence Day he was about to be put on the auction block, where he would be sold to a cotton planter. He would be forced to pick cotton, as millions of other slaves did.

For over 250 years, slaves born in Africa, and their American-born children, grandchildren, and great-grandchildren, worked at many kinds of labor. From as far north as Quebec to the southern tip of Florida, their backbreaking work built new lands and made many people rich by their skill, their talent, and their sweat.

As Europeans began to settle in the New World, it seemed that there were never enough hands to clear the land of trees, to plant and harvest, or to do the time-consuming and difficult household work. Skilled blacksmiths and carpenters, to manufacture everything from nails to ships, were in short supply.

Many Europeans who could not find jobs at home came to North America as indentured servants, bound to their employers for a certain number of years. Some were promised a little money or land at the end of their contracts, but most received only free transportation across the sea. Their lives were far from easy, and some were sold to strangers who bought their contracts. But at least they knew they would be freed when their term of service ended.

Some Africans were among those indentured servants, but most arrived as chattel slaves, the property of their masters for life. They could be sold or passed from one generation to another. They would never be free again.

Slaves and their owners often worked side by side, and some owners, like the Bennett family in Virginia, even helped their slaves gain freedom. The Bennetts bought Anthony Johnson, identified in official documents as "Antonio a Negro," in Jamestown in 1621. While he was still a slave, they let him keep his own farm and cattle, marry, and baptize his children. When Johnson became free, he became a slave owner himself, and his slave, John Casar, also owned cattle. However, Johnson did not treat Casar as generously as the Bennetts had treated him. When Casar asked for his freedom, Johnson said no.

In those early years, black slaves and black and white indentured servants all worked and socialized together, sometimes along with their owners. But not everybody approved. A white widow traveling through Connecticut in 1704 wrote disapprovingly in her diary that farmers were too "familiar" with their slaves. Some let their slaves sit at the "table and eat with them (as they say to save time) and into the dish goes the black hoof as freely as the white hand," she wrote. Her obnoxious view would become all too common among whites as the years went by.

Indentured servitude began to die out in the mid-eighteenth century, and slavery became the usual practice. As early as 1688, Quakers met in Germantown, Pennsylvania, where they held the first public protest against slavery. But most white Americans saw slavery as a normal part of life, and the demand for slaves remained high.

Snatched from Home

Six-year-old Broteer, the son of a prince of the West African Dukandarra people, was hiding in tall reeds with his mother when enemy warriors from another African state arrived. They had already threatened to attack the Dukandarra unless they were given cattle and money, and Broteer's father had agreed. But the invaders had no intention of sticking to the bargain. Broteer watched his father try in vain to fight them off. The memory of what happened next was still vivid to him in 1793, when he was nearly seventy years old.

> The very first salute I had from them was a violent blow on the head with the fore part of a gun, and at the same time a grasp round the neck. I then had a rope put about my neck, as had all the women in the thicket with me, and [we] were immediately led to my father, who was likewise pinioned and haltered for leading.

Bound and helpless, the captives were forced to carry heavy loads — Broteer's was a grindstone he carried on his head — and to follow the enemy army. At

The first African slaves arrived in America in 1619 on a Dutch warship. A Virginia colonist wrote to London that the ship was in desperate need of supplies, and had nothing to sell "but 20 and odd Negroes" that the governor and merchant bought in exchange for food.

NEW HOME, NEW NAME

Owners considered it their right to name their slaves. The name might sound mighty, like "Hercules," the Greek hero, or silly, like "Jumper." Either way, it was humiliating. There was little point in objecting, but an occasional slave did.

Lazarus La Baron already owned three slaves, Pompey, Phyllis, and Prince, when he bought Quasho. La Baron tried naming him Julius Caesar, but no matter how often his owner whipped him, starved him, or tried to bribe him, his new slave would not answer to any name but Quasho. La Baron finally let him keep his name.

William Wells Brown did not get his name back until he ran away. When he was a slave his master's nephew, also named William, arrived to live with the family. His master decided that a slave couldn't have the same name as a member of his family, and ordered Brown's mother to rename him. Brown later wrote, "This, at the time, I thought to be one of the most cruel acts that could be committed upon my rights; and I received several very severe whippings for telling people that my name was William, after orders were given to change it." For years he was known as Sandford. When he escaped, he took back his name and added "Wells Brown" to honor a man who had helped him flee.

their first stop, the warriors stabbed and beat Broteer's father to death as the boy watched in helpless horror.

Finally they came to a castle on the west coast, possibly Cape Coast Castle in today's Ghana. This was no stately, beautiful castle; slave castles were bleak, dreary, and terrifying. The captives were locked in cold, dark dungeons, sometimes for months, until ships arrived to take them to their new lives as slaves.

Although borders have changed over the years, Broteer's home was probably in what is now Mali. If so, the small child's long, hard march would have totaled about six hundred miles (almost 1,000 km), with that heavy weight on his head.

The slave traders put Broteer on a ship bound for Rhode Island, a British colony that later became one of the original thirteen states of the United States. Robert Mumford, the ship's steward, paid a trader four gallons of rum and a piece of calico cloth for the child, renamed him Venture, and took him home to New York.

Venture began a life of unceasing toil. At the age of nine he had to pound a great pile of corn each night to feed the poultry the next day. If he didn't produce enough, he was "vigorously punished," he later said.

Slaving Indoors and Out

Venture's hard life was typical. Everywhere, slaves cooked, cleaned, mended clothes, and toted water long distances from a river or a well. But most slaves worked the land. They chopped wood, cleared fields, planted crops, and did many of the tasks needed to grow rice, indigo, tobacco, and later cotton.

At first, southern planters had little success farming rice, but they discovered that slaves from the rice-growing regions of Africa like the Gold Coast or Gambia knew how to produce good crops. The Africans' know-how was so valuable to the planters that demand for slaves skyrocketed, and by 1720 the vast majority of people living in South Carolina were slaves. They brought with them not only planting techniques but also familiarity with tools like the fanner basket, which simplified the job of removing the husk from the rice kernel.

Thanks to the slaves' knowledge and skills, Americans developed a taste for rice – which they still have today – and their owners became rich. A European visitor left a record of the terrible things she witnessed. "There is no living near [the rice fields] with the putrid water that must lie on it, and the labour required for it is only fit for slaves, and I think the hardest work I have seen them engaged in," she wrote. She was right. Rice cultivation was grueling. Slaves began sowing in April, and throughout the scorching hot summer months they stood barefoot and hatless in water-soaked rice fields infested with snakes, alligators, and disease-carrying mosquitoes.

Each workday was long, although rice planters began to use the "task system," letting slaves stop work when their tasks were done. The rest of their time was their own. Slaves could use the precious bits of time to grow their own crops or make goods they could sell. But the task system did not guarantee a short workday. Often, after a full day in the fields, slaves (usually women) still had to shake the rice in the fanner baskets to remove the husks.

Even after the harvest, work went on. Slaves spent all winter preparing the fields for the next year's crop. A visitor to South Carolina wrote, "The cultivation of rice was described to me as by far the most unhealthy work in which the slaves were employed; and, in spite of every care, . . . they sank under it in great numbers." It is hard to imagine what he meant by "every care." Work in the rice fields was a job no white person would want, and no black either, but the slaves had no choice.

After he was free, Venture gave himself the last name "Smith." That name and his history appear on his gravestone, a stop along a historic route in Connecticut known as the Freedom Trail. It says Smith was the son of a king and was "kidnapped and sold as a slave but by his own industry he acquired money to purchase his freedom."

TO BE SOLD, on board the Ship *Bance-Island*, on tuesday the 6th of *May* next, at *Ashley-Ferry*; a choice cargo of about 250 fine healthy NEGROES, just arrived from the Windward & Rice Coast. —The utmost care has already been taken, and shall be continued, to keep them free from the least danger of being infected with the SMALL-POX, no boat having been on board, and all other communication with people from *Charles-Town* prevented. *Austin, Laurens, & Appleby.*

N. B. Full one Half of the above Negroes have had the SMALL-POX in their own Country.

This newspaper advertisement from about 1780 announced that 250 slaves from the Windward and Rice coasts would be sold aboard the ship *Bance Island*. By insisting that they took the "utmost care" to keep the "Negroes" free of smallpox, the traders hoped to charge a higher price.

Early Resistance

For slaves who found the rare chance to escape, the swamps and forests of South Carolina offered so many hiding places that runaways were able to form maroon communities, as they had in Surinam and Jamaica. Whenever they could, plantation slaves helped them by smuggling out tools and clothing, and the runaways hunted, fished, and grew their own food. Other runaways found welcome among Native Americans. For example, the family of Anthony Johnson — that Virginia ex-slave who refused to free his own slave — eventually lived with the Nanticoke people.

The slaveholders' greatest dread was slave rebellion, and that came to pass in South Carolina in 1739. Twenty slaves broke into a store near the Stono River, southwest of Charleston. Under the leadership of a slave named Jemmy, they killed two shopkeepers, stole weapons, and burned plantations, all the while beating drums, flying a banner, and shouting, "Liberty!" Their plan was to flee South Carolina and gain freedom in Florida, which was still Spanish territory. The group gathered more recruits and killed more whites along the way. Many of the rebels had been soldiers in Africa before they were captured and brought to South Carolina. They knew how to fight.

Armed planters caught most of the rebels within a week, although some managed to escape to Florida. But the end of the revolt did not ease the whites' minds. They feared that more rebellions would come, and they were right.

Just two years after the Stono Rebellion, a group of slaves and whites was suspected of planning a revolt in New York. They were tried for conspiracy. At the trial, they spoke about their desire simply to take a walk, dance, and go out with their friends. They did not win over the jury. Four whites and at least sixteen blacks were hanged, thirteen slaves were burned alive, and seventy were sold into slavery in the Caribbean. The government took steps to prevent further revolts. Slaves had been meeting their friends at night or at public water pumps, but New York passed a law that limited their travel. Visits to friends or family were also forbidden.

To prevent rebellion, South Carolina enacted the harsh Negro Act. Not only did it forbid slaves from meeting one another outside their plantations, but it dictated the smallest details of their lives, including what clothes they could wear and what fabrics they could use. A white person who killed a black would be fined, but a slave could be executed for killing a white, planning a revolt, conspiring to run away, committing arson, making poisons, or teaching another slave about poison.

A few sections of the law may actually have made life a little easier for slaves. Owners faced penalties if they didn't provide sufficient food, clothing, and shelter for their slaves, if they didn't give them Sundays off, or if they made them work more than fifteen hours a day during the hottest time of the year.

No matter how they tried, slaveholders on plantations or in cities could not stamp out traces of the lives slaves had lived in Africa, and they couldn't stop their slaves from having friendships, especially with those who knew their native language and customs. What a comfort that must have been to people longing for home. Slaves tried in many ways to keep their connection to their homelands. Many of them built their houses to resemble African huts with thatched roofs or clay walls. Sue Snow, a slave born in Alabama, said her mother wanted a dirt-covered floor like the ones she had known in Africa, and refused the floorboards that other slaves had.

Some slave traditions became popular with both whites and blacks. Christmas was a day of celebration in many slave households, but not always because of the religious holiday. It was also the occasion for the John Canoe festivities – fancy costumes, music, and parades. Some historians think the celebration began in West Africa, but no one is sure.

In Edenton, North Carolina, slaves from neighboring plantations marched through the town playing homemade instruments, wearing cows' tails, horns, and other costumes, and partying, said former slave Harriet Jacobs:

> For a month previous they are composing songs, which are sung on this occasion. These companies, of a hundred each, turn out early in the morning, and are allowed to go round till twelve o'clock, begging for contributions. Not a door is left unvisited where there is the least chance of obtaining a penny or a glass of rum. They do not drink while they are out, but carry the rum home in jugs, to have a carousal. These Christmas donations frequently amount to twenty or thirty dollars. It is seldom that any white man or child refuses to give them a trifle.

IN GULLAH COUNTRY

The slaves who lived on the Sea Islands off South Carolina had come from the part of Africa that is now Sierra Leone and Liberia. Their language became known as Gullah, perhaps after the Gola people from that region. Because the slaves were isolated, they managed to keep the words of their homeland alive. Some familiar words like *yam* and *tote* probably came from the Gullah language.

A BORING JOB

In 1802, when Austin Steward was an eight-year-old house slave, his job was to wait in his owner's house all day and into the night in case anyone wanted to send him on an errand. He could not sit if a member of the family was in the room. Sometimes he stood behind his master's chair for an entire day, Steward recalled in a narrative he later wrote. What torture that must have been for an energetic child!

BAND of the JAW-BONE JOHN-CANOE.

Kingston Jamaica — Aug. 1837.

John Canoe parades were popular in North Carolina, the Bahamas, and Jamaica. In this Jamaican band, the man in the center is drumming on a goatskin stretched over a wooden frame. The man on the left is playing a rasp made from the lower jaw of a horse, creating a rattling noise by running a piece of wood back and forth over the teeth.

Jacobs's owner told his daughter that John Canoe was the highlight of Christmas in 1838. Without these celebrations, he wrote, Christmas "would have passed without the least manifestation of mirth, cheerful joy, or hilarity."

John Canoe celebrations must have been bittersweet for slaves. New Year's Day, just a week away, was the traditional day when they were bought and sold, and for some of them, Christmas would be their last happy time together. "Were it not that hiring day is near at hand, and many families are fearfully looking forward to the probability of separation in a few days," Jacobs wrote, "Christmas might be a happy season for the poor slaves."

Thoughts of Equality

Because eighteenth-century America was not yet a country, colonists from Massachusetts in the north right down to South Carolina still thought of themselves as British, but many were outraged by the way the British government treated them. The "mother country" needed money, and tried to get it by taxing the colonists. Colonists railed against "taxation without representation" because they were asked to pay British taxes without having a vote in the British Parliament. A slaveholder in Philadelphia wrote, "Those who are taxed without their own consent . . . are slaves!" Other colonists took up the cry, declaring that they would not be "slaves" to Britain, and demanding equality with their fellow citizens across the ocean.

Blacks, and some whites, too, thought the colonists' arguments should apply to slavery. In 1773, slaves in Massachusetts went to the legislature to ask for their liberty, saying, "We have no Property! We have no Wives! No children! We have no City! No Country!" but "in common with all other men we have a natural right to our freedoms." The delegates were not won over.

Others used religion as an argument against slavery. In 1700, Samuel Sewall, a respected judge, had published *The Selling of Joseph: A Memorial* to show that the Bible condemns the buying and selling of human beings. People in Sewall's time found verses in the Bible to justify slavery as well, but Sewall refused to read the

Bible that way, or to excuse slavery as a means of saving Africans' souls by making them Christians. "Evil must not be done, that good may come of it," he said, and since capturing Africans separated husbands from wives, and parents from children, he considered it a great evil.

When people excused slavery because the captives had been taken from their homes by Africans in a lawful war, Sewall denied that a war to take captives could be lawful, and said that those who bought slaves were as guilty as the people who had captured them. He reminded his readers that the Bible taught them to treat others as they themselves wished to be treated because God made all people of "One Blood."

The American Revolution

Liberty was increasingly on the colonists' minds. By the 1760s, colonists who were demanding more rights were known as Patriots. Those who wanted to remain subjects of Britain were known as Loyalists. Patriot anger turned explosive in April 1775, when a British armed force and members of a local militia exchanged gunfire in Lexington, Massachusetts. Eight Patriots died. It was the first battle in the colonists' war for independence from Britain, the American Revolution.

In May 1775, Patriots sent delegates from each of the colonies to Philadelphia for a meeting they called the Second Continental Congress (the first had met just a year earlier). The congress was to manage the war effort for the Patriots, and it named George Washington the commander in chief of the Continental Army. On July 2, 1776, while the war was still raging, the congress declared the colonies' independence, and two days later it issued a written Declaration of Independence. The declaration expressed the colonists' grievances against Britain and the rights due to the people, including "life, liberty, and the pursuit of happiness." Fifty-six delegates signed the document, and they are among the statesmen known as the Founders.

Most of America's Founders knew that slavery was wrong, but many were slave owners themselves. George Washington bought and sold slaves before the Revolution, until he had something of a change of heart. He refused to sell any of his slaves or even hire them out, and in 1799, he wrote to a nephew that he was "principled against this kind of traffic in the human species. To hire them out is almost as bad because they could not be disposed of in families to any advantage, and to disperse the families I have an aversion." Washington didn't free

Washington as a Farmer was painted more than fifty years after the president's death, when there was more opposition to slavery. The artist portrays Washington favorably by showing his slaves as contented and well dressed and doing leisurely work, with refreshments handy.

his slaves in his lifetime or even when he died. In his will he directed that they be freed after his wife died. Thomas Jefferson, who wrote "All men are created equal" in the Declaration of Independence, freed only eight of his many slaves in his lifetime and did not free the rest in his will. And though he was against the *international* slave trade, he sold many of his own slaves within the country.

Another prominent colonist, the Massachusetts lawyer James Otis Jr., owned slaves but still wrote, "The colonists are by the law of nature freeborn, as indeed all men are, white or black. . . . Does it follow that 'tis right to enslave a man because he is black? . . . It is a clear truth that those who every day barter away other men's liberty will soon care little for their own. . . ."

The Founders were used to lives of privilege and ease, and to give up the slaves who made their comfortable lives possible would be "inconvenient," to quote Patrick Henry, a Virginian who supported the revolution. He said that every thinking honest man opposed slavery in principle, but not in practice. When colonists spoke about the equality of men, they were not thinking of blacks or of women. They meant that they wanted the same rights as men of their rank in Britain. They were not willing to give up any of their property, which included slaves.

Both the Loyalists and the Patriots were short of troops, and both sides enlisted blacks to fight. More blacks joined the Loyalists because the British promised them freedom. The British governor of Virginia, Lord Dunmore, reasoned that black labor and troops would strengthen the Loyalist side, and their flight would rob Patriots of their slave labor force. On November 14, 1775, he issued a proclamation declaring "all indented servants, Negroes, or others . . . free, that are able and willing to bear arms."

In the end probably only eight hundred black men joined Lord Dunmore's Ethiopian Regiment, whose uniforms proclaimed, "Liberty to Slaves." As word spread that Dunmore had offered freedom, around a hundred thousand slaves escaped behind British lines.

The Patriots also talked of promising freedom to slaves who fought for them, but in the end the colonies of South Carolina and Georgia blocked the offer. They were afraid that the slave system would collapse.

One of the most famous black soldiers, Colonel Tye, ran away from his cruel master the day after Dunmore's proclamation and joined the Ethiopian Regiment. He knew where the swamps and creeks were, and his troops, both black and white, stole supplies and freed slaves in raids against the Patriots in New York and New Jersey. The British recognized his bravery by calling him *captain* and then *colonel*, although the titles weren't official – because he was black. Tye died in action, but his regiment fought until the end of the war.

In September 1783, Britain and the former colonies signed a peace treaty, ending the war. An independent nation, the United States of America, was born.

Freedom for Some

Boston King was a fugitive slave who served with the British forces. He made his way to New York after the war, and later wrote that runaways had been desperate because of news they had heard:

Black and white soldiers fought side by side in many battles. One officer said, "The Negro can take the field instead of his master, and therefore [in every regiment there are] Negroes in abundance and among them are able-bodied and strong fellows." These men are dressed in uniforms of the 1770s.

> All the slaves, in number 2000, were to be delivered up to their masters, altho' some of them had been three or four years among the English. This dreadful rumour filled us all with inexpressible anguish and terror, especially when we saw our old masters coming from Virginia, North Carolina, and other parts, and seizing upon their slaves in the streets of New York, or even dragging them out of their beds. Many of the slaves had very cruel masters, so that the thoughts of returning home with them embittered life to us. For some days we lost our appetite for food, and sleep departed from our eyes.

The rumor had some truth to it. Owners petitioned Congress to have runaways returned to them; others spent large amounts to bribe policemen to turn their former slaves over to them, or to hire agents to find them. But Sir Guy Carleton, the commander in chief of the British forces in the colonies, kept Lord Dunmore's promise to free blacks who had crossed over to British lines.

The British evacuated King and his wife and about four thousand other former slaves to their colony of Nova Scotia in Canada. But when they got there, the evacuees did not find the welcome they had hoped for. The Nova Scotians cheated them out of good land, mobs attacked them, and people drove them from their homes. Still hoping for a better life, the Kings joined a group of blacks who traveled to West Africa and settled in a colony in Sierra Leone in 1792.

Law of the Land

The new American nation required new laws. George Washington presided when delegates met in Philadelphia in 1787 to enact a constitution. Laws on slavery were the most controversial they discussed. Some delegates wanted to ban slavery outright, others wanted to limit the slave trade, and still others wanted no restrictions. Delegates from South Carolina and Georgia declared that their states would not join the union if slavery was abolished.

The framers decided to avoid the word "slavery." It does not appear anywhere in the Constitution. Instead, they protected the institution of slavery by saying that a "Person held to Service or Labour" in one state would remain in service, and must be returned to his or her owner. This meant that a runaway slave could not become free by fleeing to territory that banned slavery. Individual states could ban slavery, but the federal Constitution allowed it to continue.

Elizabeth Freeman, a Massachusetts slave, had heard talk about the new constitution of the state of Massachusetts, which said that "all men are born free and equal." One day in 1781, after her mistress struck her with a heated kitchen shovel, Freeman stalked out of the house, determined to claim her rights in court. When her master tried to get her back, she approached a lawyer, Theodore Sedgwick. Sedgwick went to court on behalf of Freeman as well as another of the owner's slaves, known today only as Brom. A jury ruled in their favor. When another Massachusetts slave claimed his freedom, Chief Justice William Cushing concluded in his trial notes that "there can be no such thing as perpetual servitude of a rational Creature," and instructed the jury that slavery was unconstitutional in Massachusetts. Slavery ended there in 1783. By 1804, all northern states would have laws abolishing slavery, either immediately or gradually.

Slave owners in the other states were jittery. The slave revolt in St-Domingue in 1791 was fresh in their minds and they had not forgotten those earlier American slave revolts. Now they feared something worse. Word traveled fast, even in those days. Owners knew their slaves would hear about the successful Caribbean revolt, and they were certain it would give them ideas.

It did. In Virginia, in 1800, an elaborate conspiracy led by blacksmith Gabriel Prosser was uncovered. The plan was to march on the capital, Richmond, seize weapons, take white officials hostage, and negotiate the slaves' freedom. The plot was thwarted when two slaves panicked and confessed. Prosser and twenty-five other slaves were hanged for conspiracy.

The Country Grows

In 1803, the United States bought a vast amount of territory from the French. Known as the Louisiana Purchase, the land extended the United States to the southwest and doubled its size. This was prime land for growing cotton, and for that, planters demanded slaves.

By 1789, Congress had banned slavery from the country's northwest region but not from the southwest. This meant that, as new territories became states, some would allow slaves and others would not. Most of the land in the Louisiana Purchase was in the south, where the newly arrived cotton planters could bring their slaves.

While the country was growing, trouble with Britain resurfaced. Arguments over trade and territory led to the War of 1812, which was fought from as far north as Canada, which was British at the time, to as far south as Louisiana. As in the Revolution, some slaves aided the British in hopes of gaining their freedom. General Andrew Jackson offered slaves freedom and the same pay as whites if they would join him on the American side in battle in New Orleans, Louisiana.

James Roberts was one of the recruits. With little training in warfare, he and the other slaves marched three hundred miles (480 km) from Natchez, Mississippi, to join Jackson's army in New Orleans. When they spotted the British soldiers, Roberts was terrified, with good reason. The British troops outnumbered the Americans, and they were better trained. Before the battle began, according to Roberts, Jackson was unsure how to proceed. One of the black soldiers suggested building a fort of cotton bales with portholes to shoot through, and even

COTTON TAKES OVER

An invention can change the course of history, and the cotton gin (short for "engine") did just that. When Eli Whitney traveled to Georgia in 1793, he saw that the work of removing clean cotton from the seed pods took so long that few farmers wanted to tackle the crop. He designed a machine that would make it easier and cheaper to produce cotton, just when people in the North and in Europe wanted more cotton cloth. New cotton plantations were created – bringing wealth to plantation owners and textile manufacturers, but not to the slaves who produced the crop.

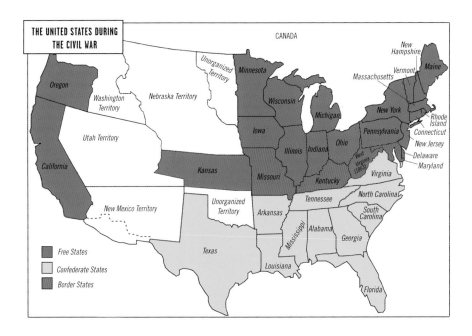

The war ended in 1815. The British left but slavery remained. In just ten years, between 1810 and 1820, slave traders shipped approximately 120,000 slaves to Alabama, Mississippi, and Louisiana. In 1819, Alabama joined the union as a slave state, giving the country eleven slave states and eleven free. Missouri was to join the union that same year. Would it be slave or free? Northern members of Congress refused to admit it as a slave state, but the southern states wanted slavery. The

supervised the construction. Jackson's troops quickly defeated the British. Roberts lost the forefinger of his left hand and suffered a head wound, but later he was dealt an even harsher blow – Jackson denied him his freedom. "You are not my property, and I cannot take another man's property and set it free," said the general. Roberts felt betrayed, and later explained:

> [It] was by the indomitable bravery of the colored men that the battle was fought and victory gained. Had there been less bravery with us, the British would have gained the victory, and in that event they would have set the slaves free; so that I now can see how we, in that war, contributed to fasten our chains tighter.

stalemate was broken by the Missouri Compromise (1820), which let Missouri be a slave state but banned slavery from other states north of Missouri's southern border. Now the country was divided into two parts – the North, where slavery was illegal, and the South, where it was about to become even more deeply entrenched. Rice was being replaced by a new and demanding crop – cotton.

Slave owners and overseers had the power to make their slaves' lives bearable or unbearable. Solomon Northup had both a cruel owner and a cruel overseer. When he was finally free, he described his life on a cotton plantation:

> The day's work over in the field, the baskets are "toted," carried to the gin-house, where the cotton is weighed. No matter how fatigued and weary he may be – no matter how much he longs for sleep and rest – a slave never approaches the gin-house with his basket of cotton but with fear. If it falls short in weight – if he has not performed the full task appointed him, he knows that he must suffer.

Slaves who picked too little were whipped. Those who picked more than the expected amount could suffer too, because the owner would expect that larger weight the next day. Pity the poor slaves who did not meet that new quota, because they would be whipped. After the overseer weighed the cotton, the slaves' work would continue:

> This done, the labor of the day is not yet ended, by any means. Each one must then attend to his respective chores. One feeds the mules, another, the swine – another cuts the wood, and so forth; besides, the packing is all done by candle light. Finally, at a late hour, they reach the quarters, sleepy and overcome with the long day's toil. Then a fire must be kindled in the cabin, the corn ground in the small hand-mill, and supper, and dinner for the next day in the field, prepared. All that is allowed them is corn and bacon, which is given out at the corncrib and smoke-house every Sunday morning. Each one receives, as his weekly allowance, three and a half pounds of bacon [about 1.5 kilos], and corn enough to make a peck [about 9 liters] of meal. That is all – no tea, coffee, sugar, and with the exception of a very scanty sprinkling now and then, no salt.

KIDNAPPED FROM THE NORTH

There was so much money to be made from slave trading that any black was in danger of being looked at as a potential slave. Solomon Northup had been born free in New York State, but in 1841 two white men promised him a job, and he left his wife and children to go with them to Washington, D.C., for work. But there was no job — Northup had been kidnapped. The men sold him to traders who took him to Louisiana.

It was twelve long years before he found someone to help. A white carpenter from Canada who was working on the plantation mailed a letter from Northup to his friends back home. The letter was sent in mid-August and Northup waited anxiously all through the summer and fall, past Christmas, and into the new year. He had no way of knowing if his letter had reached its destination, if his friends would help, or even if they were still alive. Finally, Henry B. Northup, whose father had owned and then freed Solomon's father, arrived in Louisiana with documents from the governor of New York and other authorities to prove that Northup was a free man.

Slaves tried to ease one another's burden whenever they could. A former slave in Virginia said his grandmother was so small that she could never pick enough cotton to meet the quota. The other slaves liked her, so they would put some of their cotton into her bucket to help her. Still, they could do only so much, and sometimes she came up short. "Grandma said that often she was whipped until she could barely grunt."

Lightening the Burden

After exhausting workdays, slaves grasped at any chance to relax. Most masters didn't want them to socialize on weeknights, when they thought they should be resting for the next day's work. One Virginia owner said they should be forced to work hard or "they become restive, run about at night for want of exercise in the day, to pilfer, and visit, hear the news, etc. etc." That didn't suppress the slaves' very human need for some pleasure. "Might whip us the next day," said Charles Grandy, a former slave in Virginia, "but we done had our dance."

Saturday night was a different matter, because there was no work on Sunday. Slaves could gather for singing and dancing to the music of instruments they made from objects they found — a sheep's rib or cow's jaw, a piece of iron, a hollow gourd, or horsehair, according to a former slave in Texas. "They'd take the buffalo horn and scrape it out to make the flute," he said. Sometimes their owners provided food for them, but most of the time they just shared whatever they had.

On many plantations, slaves could choose their own activities on Sunday. The slaveholders may have hoped they would rest up for the workweek ahead, but many of them understood that they were more likely to get good workers if they gave the slaves some time to themselves. Some owners allowed visiting on neighboring plantations. William Wells Brown wrote that he and the other slaves spent Sundays hunting, fishing, and making brooms and baskets — but that changed when their master "got religion," and required his slaves to attend family worship.

Reading and Religion

At first, most owners did not want their slaves to have any religion, and certainly not one they brought with them from Africa. But as years passed, it occurred to them that spoken instruction in the Christian faith would both control the slaves' behavior and save their souls.

The owners may have thought religion would teach slaves obedience to their masters, but instead slaves found solace in biblical stories like Exodus, the tale of how Moses led the Hebrew slaves out of Egypt. A slave in Texas wrote that his owner did not like the slaves attending religious meetings, but they found a way to do so anyway. While they worked during the day, someone might start singing the song "Stealing Away to Jesus." To the overseer that would be just another song, but it told the slaves that there would be a religious meeting that evening. They would meet out of view of the owners, and sing and pray all night.

Few owners wanted their slaves to learn to read, and many Southern states passed laws against teaching them. Reading anything – even the Bible – could give them dangerous new ideas. But the young slave Frederick Bailey was eager to learn to read, and his mistress was eager to teach him.

Hugh and Sophia Auld had brought Frederick to their Baltimore house to be a companion for their little son, Tommy. Sophia Auld liked to read the Bible to the children. Intrigued by the mystery of converting marks on a page to spoken words, Frederick plucked up the courage to ask her to teach him to read. He caught on quickly, learning to spell out words of three or four letters. Sophia was so proud of her young pupil that, when her husband stepped into the room, she showed off Frederick's accomplishments to him. To her surprise, he was far from pleased, saying:

> If he learns to read the Bible it will forever unfit him to be a slave. He should know nothing but the will of his master, and learn to obey it. . . . Learning will do him no good, . . . making him disconsolate and unhappy. If you teach him how to read, he'll want to know to write, and this accomplished, he'll be running away with himself.

This event changed Frederick's life. If Auld was right and knowledge would make him unfit to be a slave, then he was determined to read. When he grew up, he escaped to the North under the name he chose for himself – Frederick Douglass – and became a fierce opponent of slavery.

More Slave Resistance

The bloodiest slave revolt in United States history happened in Virginia in 1831. Nat Turner and six other slaves killed five whites at the plantation where he was enslaved. Turner believed he had a sign from God to lead the attack. "I saw white spirits and black spirits engaged in battle, and the sun darkened – thunder rolled in the heavens, and blood flowed in the streams," he explained later, when he was in jail. Turner gained followers as he went from plantation to plantation, until approximately sixty of them had killed about sixty whites, mostly women and children. The state's militia captured most of the slaves, but Turner hid out for sixty-eight days before he was caught and hanged.

The rebellion so terrorized whites that they went on rampages throughout the South to uncover other plots of rebellion, and to intimidate blacks so they would never again rise up in revolt. Free blacks as well as slaves were at the mercy of whites. Harriet Jacobs's grandmother was free in North Carolina, but her home was searched, her letters were ripped up, her clothes were stolen, and her garden uprooted. Blacks who lived on the outskirts of town were in the most danger. A ragtag gang of whites, emboldened by a little power, would storm into their homes, scattering buckshot so that searchers could find it and claim it was proof that they were rebels. They whipped men, women, and children "till the blood stood in puddles at their feet," Jacobs wrote.

For another two weeks the outrages continued, with beatings, searches, and arrests. The authorities had to keep a group of blacks in jail to protect them from the white mob until the capture of Nat Turner helped to quell the whites' rage.

Once again, rebellion resulted in stricter laws. In Virginia, blacks could no longer hold religious meetings at night unless they had written permission from their masters or overseers. New laws prohibited the teaching of reading and writing to slaves. In 1834, the state banned free blacks from entering Virginia, in case they stirred up trouble. Slave owners in Virginia had reason to worry. They might have defeated Nat Turner, but slaves would continue to fight for three more decades, in the North and in the South.

This print portrays several scenes from the Nat Turner rebellion. Turner said in his confession that a "Spirit" had inspired him to fulfill Christ's prophecy that "the last shall be first, and the first last." To him, this meant that the time had come when Christ would lift up the downtrodden slaves.

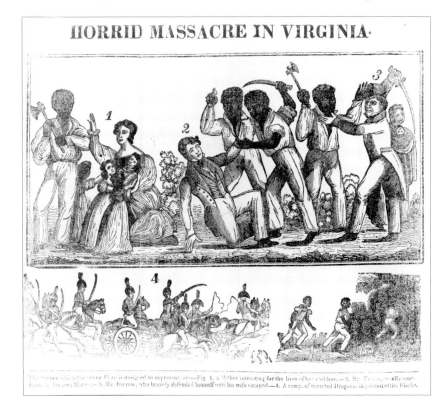

CHAPTER 10
CIVIL WAR, CIVIL RIGHTS: THE UNITED STATES

When David Walker was growing up in North Carolina at the end of the eighteenth century, he saw black slaves abused by their white masters. David was a free black man, and his anger toward slavery grew and grew, until he realized he would have to leave the South. "I cannot remain where I must hear slaves' chains," he said.

After he moved north, he published one of the most radical antislavery pamphlets written in America, *An Appeal to the Colored Citizens of the World*. Walker refused to accept anything less than immediate abolition. He said that America was "more our country than . . . the whites'" because "The greatest riches in all America have risen from our blood and tears." Walker even praised the Haitian revolution ("the glory of blacks and terror of tyrants") and warned Americans that the day would come when their own slaves would rise up, unless they were freed. His words frightened Southerners, who banned his pamphlet and set a price on his head. To get his words to the slaves, he smuggled copies to his fellow used-clothing dealers in the South.

By 1830, there were fewer than three thousand slaves living in the North, but life was far from easy for free blacks like David Walker. Some states passed laws denying black men the right to vote, others restricted where blacks could live. And as English, Scottish, and Irish immigrants began to arrive in America looking for work, they saw free blacks as rivals for jobs, and anti-black riots broke out.

Northern blacks fought back. They organized the Colored Convention Movement to fight against discrimination and slavery and founded America's first black newspaper, *Freedom's Journal*.

William Lloyd Garrison

One of the most famous antislavery publications, *The Liberator*, was the work of a white man, William Lloyd Garrison. He was America's most important white abolitionist.

Early American abolitionists were split into two camps. One worked to set up a colony for blacks in Africa, and the other wanted to pass laws that would free slaves over time, on the model of the Northern states. Garrison didn't like either idea.

What's more, he called the United States Constitution a "covenant with death," because it permitted the capture of runaways and gave the South immense power in Congress. To make his point, Garrison burned a copy of the Constitution at an Independence Day speech in 1854. He even wanted the North to secede from the Union so it would not share the South's guilt for holding slaves. "No Union with slaveholders" was his slogan. Garrison moved the abolition movement away from gradual emancipation and toward freeing slaves immediately.

Garrison founded the American Anti-Slavery Society and wrote its Declaration of Sentiments, which echoed the words of the Declaration of Independence, "all men are created equal." He may have sounded like a firebrand, but he remained a firm pacifist. He wanted to end slavery by changing public opinion, not by violence.

Sixty abolitionists from New England, Pennsylvania, New York State, and Ohio attended the first meeting of the American Anti-Slavery Society in 1833. Most were religious and some, who were very rich, gave money to the movement. Quaker women soon formed their own group, the Philadelphia Female Anti-Slavery Society. Three black delegates attended, and African Americans later formed their own societies.

Anti-Abolition Anger Erupts

The abolitionists paid agents to travel throughout the North, organize meetings, establish local antislavery societies, and speak publicly. In 1835 they launched the "great postal campaign," mailing over a million antislavery pamphlets to ministers, elected officials, and newspapers. All this made supporters of slavery furious. In Charleston a mob broke into the post office, carted off the antislavery mail, and used it to start a bonfire to burn Garrison in effigy.

Even in the North abolitionists were persecuted. Those who were profiting from slavery, like owners of cotton mills, sometimes encouraged the violence. In Utica, New York, lawyers, politicians, merchants, and bankers, together with a crowd of workers, roughly broke up a state convention of abolitionists. In Boston, Garrison himself was dragged through the streets by a crowd. In Philadelphia, a mob became so disruptive during a speech by Southern abolitionist Angelina Grimké Weld that she challenged the protesters:

What is a mob? What would the breaking of every window be? Any evidence that we are wrong, or that slavery is a good and wholesome institution? What if the mob should burst in upon us, break up our meeting and commit violence upon our persons – would this be anything compared to what the slaves endure?

Weld was speaking on May 15, 1838, at the Anti-Slavery Convention of American Women. The event was held at Pennsylvania Hall, a building constructed with funds raised by abolitionists and dedicated just the day before as a meeting place. Three thousand people, black and white, were there to hear her when a mob outside threw stones at the windows and tried to shout her down. Undaunted, Weld urged women, who could not yet vote, to run a petition campaign, as Englishwomen had done. At the end of her speech, whites and blacks left Pennsylvania Hall arm in arm to protect the black women against the rocks and insults awaiting them. The nervous mayor asked the organizers to ban black women from the next day's meeting. When they refused, he locked the doors and announced to the mob outside that the meeting had been canceled.

Encouraged by this victory, the mob turned on the building with a vengeance, setting it on fire. When firefighters arrived, they protected only the buildings surrounding Pennsylvania Hall, not the hall itself. Any firefighters who tried to protect Pennsylvania Hall got hosed themselves.

Abolitionists may not have found the welcome they had expected in the North, but they were certainly attracting publicity. This brought in more wealthy supporters, people who could help to pay for newspapers, speakers, education, lawyers, and conventions.

The publicity was working. Northerners blamed Southerners for the outbursts, and came to see the Northern way of life – which they thought was based on hard work and free labor – as superior to the pampered lives of Southern planters, whom they stereotyped as lazy and decadent.

Taking Slavery to Court

On September 6, 1839, two very different men met in a jail cell in New Haven, Connecticut: Cinqué, an African, and Lewis Tappan, the wealthy co-founder of the American Anti-Slavery Society. Tappan hoped that the case of Cinqué and

This sketch was drawn while Cinqué (here called Joseph Cinquez) was awaiting trial in Connecticut. He told his fellow captives on board the *Amistad*: "I am resolved it is better to die than to be a white man's slave."

JOSEPH CINQUEZ.

forty-two other Africans awaiting trial for murder would force an American court to declare slavery illegal in the United States.

The Africans had been on board the cargo ship *Amistad*, towed into a Connecticut harbor a few days earlier. Two Spanish slave traders from the ship told a judge that the Africans were legally purchased Cuban slaves who had rebelled and killed the ship's captain and cook. Abolitionists doubted the story. They believed that the Africans had been illegally enslaved and had acted in self-defense. Tappan formed the Friends of the Amistad Africans Committee.

Tappan learned that Cinqué was the son of one of the principal men of his village. He had been captured to repay a debt, and had then been sold to an African slave trader and resold to Portuguese traders. They had put him, along with several hundred other Africans, on a slave ship to Cuba.

In Havana, he and fifty-two other kidnapped Africans had been bought by the Spanish traders, who had shipped them on the *Amistad* to Porto Principe, Cuba, to be sold. The crew had treated the captives poorly, and when the captives had asked the cook what would happen to them, he had pantomimed being killed and eaten. That was when Cinqué and some of the others decided to rebel. Cinqué found a loose nail that he used to unlock his shackles and release his companions. They found sugar-cane knives and killed the captain and the cook. Cinqué then ordered the Spanish to sail the ship eastward, back to Africa. This they did during the day, but at night the crew steered north, which was how they ended up in Connecticut.

The case worked its way up all the way to the U.S. Supreme Court. Tappan's committee managed to convince one of America's most respected citizens, former president John Quincy Adams, to take the case. The captives' lawyers had argued in the lower courts that the Africans were free because the slave trade was illegal under Spanish law, but Adams appealed to higher ideals. Justice was blind to color, he said, and this case had been tainted by "sympathy with the white, antipathy to the black" from the first. More important, "the moment you come to the Declaration of Independence, that every man has a right to life and liberty, an inalienable right, this case is decided," he said. "I ask nothing more in behalf of these unfortunate men than this Declaration." The Supreme Court agreed with the lower court that the Africans were not legally slaves. They had been kidnapped, and therefore had the right to free themselves by force.

About two and a half years after being transported from their homes to Cuba, the freed Africans, together with five white missionaries and teachers, boarded a ship to Sierra Leone, where the abolitionists hoped to establish a mission. The *Amistad* case had brought abolitionists together and had rallied many Americans against slavery. But the courts had not found that slavery itself was illegal in America. The abolitionists would have to continue their campaign.

Frederick Douglass

Frederick Douglass – the Frederick who had defied his owner by teaching himself to read and write – escaped in 1838 and made his way to New Bedford, Massachusetts, where he would be safer from slave catchers. There he met the abolitionists of the American Anti-Slavery Society, led by William Lloyd Garrison. When he first told his story at a meeting in 1841, "Flinty hearts were pierced and cold ones melted by his eloquence," one delegate said.

For four years Douglass worked with Garrison, lecturing about his life as a slave, until he published his autobiography, *A Narrative of the Life of Frederick Douglass*. Now his identity was out and he was in danger of being recaptured. To avoid that fate, he left the United States on a speaking tour of England, Scotland, Wales, and Ireland, where he met eminent writers like Hans Christian Andersen. For the first time in his life, Douglass was in a place where he experienced no racism: "I employ a cab – I am seated beside white people – I reach the hotel – I enter the same door – I am shown into the same parlor – I dine at the same table – and no one is offended. . . . When I go to church I am met by no upturned nose and scornful lip," he wrote to Garrison.

Douglass returned to America a free man in more ways than one. He was

Although most of those who attended Frederick Douglass's lectures opposed slavery, many shared the common racial prejudices of their time, and did not expect that a former slave could learn to make fine speeches. "They said I did not talk like a slave, look like a slave, or act like a slave," Douglass later wrote.

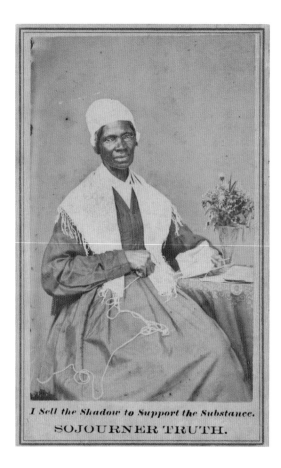

I Sell the Shadow to Support the Substance.

SOJOURNER TRUTH.

Feminists of the twentieth century were inspired by Sojourner Truth's fight for freedom, and by her stirring "Ain't I a Woman?" speech. In 2009, the United States recognized her contribution to human rights when her sculpture became the first memorial to a black woman in the Rotunda of the U.S. Capitol building in Washington, D.C.

literally free, after a group of British abolitionist sympathizers bought his freedom from his owner, ending his worries about being recaptured. He also felt free to cut his ties with Garrison and strike out on his own. He moved to Rochester, New York, where he gave blacks an independent voice by launching *The North Star* (later *Frederick Douglass's Paper*), his own antislavery newspaper.

Black abolitionists did not always see things the way Garrison and his followers did. They were often more practical and willing to compromise. Douglass had begun to look again at the American Constitution and, unlike Garrison, he thought it could be read in a way that guaranteed freedom for black Americans. While Garrison urged his followers not to vote, Douglass's paper would sometimes give support to political parties. Until he died at age seventy-seven, in 1895, Frederick Douglass dedicated his life to his people, as one of America's leading abolitionists and its most esteemed black leader of the nineteenth century.

Sojourner Truth

In 1851, a black woman strode to the pulpit of a church in Akron, Ohio, where churchmen were addressing black and white delegates to a women's rights meeting. Listening to the speakers, she heard that men have a "superior intellect," that Jesus was a man, and that "if God had desired the equality of woman, He would have given some token of His will through the birth, life, and death of the Savior."

When they had finished, the visitor, who called herself Sojourner Truth, made her way to the podium. The man who chaired the session later wrote that "every eye was fixed on this almost Amazon form, which stood nearly six feet high, head erect, and eyes piercing the upper air like one in a dream," as she spoke these words:

That man over there says that women need to be helped into carriages, and lifted over ditches, and to have the best place everywhere. Nobody ever helps me into carriages, or over mud-puddles, or gives me any best place! And ain't I a woman? Look at me! Look at my arm! I have ploughed and planted, and gathered into barns, and no man could head me! And ain't I a woman? I could work as much and eat as much as a man — when I could get it — and bear the lash as well! And ain't I a woman?

Sojourner Truth was born a slave in rural New York around 1797. Her name was then Isabella, and when she was ten years old she was auctioned away from her mother and her youngest brother. Over the years she married, had children, and was sold to a series of masters. In 1826, she escaped to freedom. By 1827, the state of New York effectively freed all its slaves. Isabella's owner had sold away Isabella's five-year-old son, Peter, who had ended up in slavery in Alabama. With courage and determination, Isabella sued in court and got Peter back. That was when she discovered how cruel Southern slavery was. Peter's body was covered with sores and scars from his master's beatings. "Sometimes I crawled under the stoop, mammy, the blood running all about me, and my back would stick to the boards," he told her.

Isabella became a traveling preacher with a new name, Sojourner Truth, saying that God had called on her to "sojourn," or travel, from camp meeting to camp meeting, speaking the truth.

In the 1860s, when North and South clashed in a bloody civil war, she worked for the National Freedmen's Relief Association, helping freed slaves find jobs. She even met President Abraham Lincoln. After the war, she refused to be put off Washington's streetcars, which were off limits to blacks, and continued to agitate for women's rights. She even attempted to vote in the 1872 presidential election, to make her point. She never gave up.

The Fugitive Slave Act of 1850

Harriet Jacobs was a young slave in the home of Dr. James Norcom of North Carolina. When she became an attractive teenager, her master began to pay more and more unwelcome attention to her. She turned to a sympathetic older white man for protection; he gave her some support, but also fathered two children with her. Meanwhile, Norcom pursued Jacobs. Desperate to escape his advances, she went into hiding. For seven years she lived in the crawl space of the house owned by her grandmother, a free woman. Through a tiny crack in the wall she could see her children play, but no one told them she was there. In 1842, when she was about twenty-nine years old, she no longer felt safe and escaped to New York City. When Norcom traveled north to find her, she fled to Boston. Ultimately she moved to Rochester, where she joined the abolitionist community. With the help of friends and her free grandmother, her children moved north as well.

In 1850, any sense of security that a runaway slave in a free state might have enjoyed vanished. Congress passed a new law that let federal marshals demand help

BLACKS' RIGHTS, WOMEN'S RIGHTS, HUMAN RIGHTS

People who supported rights for blacks did not necessarily support rights for women. When William Lloyd Garrison attended the World Anti-Slavery Convention in London with his colleague Lucretia Mott, the London organization refused to seat the American women. In protest, Garrison walked out.

Mott and another woman ejected from the London meeting, Elizabeth Cady Stanton, resolved then and there to organize a women's rights conference in America. It took eight years, but in 1848 the First Women's Rights Convention met in Seneca Falls, New York. Many of the organizers were abolitionists. Richard and Jane Hunt, for example, sheltered runaway slaves in their carriage house, and their factory produced wool cloth that people could buy to avoid using slave-made cotton.

from any citizen in capturing a slave who had escaped to the North. The Fugitive Slave Act did not permit trials for those accused of being escaped slaves, did not require proof that the person was truly a runaway, and gave a reward to people who found a supposed runaway. This meant that any white could turn in any black person as a fugitive. Anyone who helped a runaway could be imprisoned as long as six months and fined up to $1,000. For Jacobs, this new law marked "the beginning of a reign of terror to the colored population."

No longer safe in the United States, as many as twenty thousand blacks fled to Canada over the next ten years. There they would find a safe haven, because the Canadian government would not return them to slavery. In her book *Incidents in the Life of a Slave Girl*, Jacobs wrote:

> Many families, who had lived in the city for twenty years, fled from it now. Many a poor washerwoman, who, by hard labor, had made herself a comfortable home, was obliged to sacrifice her furniture, bid a hurried farewell to friends, and seek her fortune among strangers in Canada. Many a wife discovered a secret she had never known before – that her husband was a fugitive, and must leave her to insure his own safety. Worse still, many a husband discovered that his wife had fled from slavery years ago, and as "the child follows the condition of its mother," the children of his love were liable to be seized and carried into slavery. Everywhere, in those humbled homes there was consternation and anguish. But what cared the legislators of the "dominant race" for the blood they were crushing out of trampled hearts?

Fleeing Slavery

Canada had been a destination for slaves since Upper Canada (today's Ontario) became the first British colony to have a law restricting slavery. The Act for the Gradual Abolition of Slavery was passed in 1793 at the urging of the lieutenant governor, John Graves Simcoe. He couldn't get a bill for immediate abolition passed, because some Loyalist members of his executive council were slaveholders, but his act freed the children of current slaves once they reached the age of twenty-five and stated that their children would be born free. When black troops who had joined the British forces during the War of 1812 were rewarded with land, Canada's black population grew. By the 1830s, there were black settlements in Southern Ontario waiting to welcome the fugitives.

One June afternoon in 1833, an angry crowd of black people armed with pistols, knives, and even swords gathered outside a Detroit jail. Thornton Blackburn, a fugitive slave from Kentucky, was brought out of the jail in shackles. He had been living in Detroit peacefully with his wife, Lucie, when they were both arrested as runaways. He asked to speak to the crowd, and when he stepped forward, someone tossed a pistol to him. He fired it in the air. With that, the crowd surged forward, grabbing Blackburn. Pursued by a posse, bugles blaring and fire bells clanging, they spirited him away to the Rouge River in a cart owned by an elderly black man and pulled by his blind horse. A boat was waiting, but the boatman stalled until one of the rescuers bribed him with a gold watch. Then he ferried the runaway across the river to Upper Canada.

The Sunday before, two black women, Mrs. Lightfoot and Mrs. French, had asked the jailer for permission to pray with Lucie Blackburn. That evening, according to an account written at the time, they made their "sorrowful departure, tears falling like rain," their faces covered with handkerchiefs. It was only the next day that the jailer discovered Mrs.

THE BOOK THAT CHANGED HISTORY

Nineteenth-century readers were gripped by Harriet Beecher Stowe's novel *Uncle Tom's Cabin*, and wept over the slave Eliza's desperate fear of losing her baby: "[H]e was all I had . . . and, ma'am, they were going to take him away from me – to *sell* him – sell him down south, ma'am, to go all alone – a baby that had never been away from his mother in his life!"

Uncle Tom's Cabin was the blockbuster of the century. Published in 1852, it sold 10,000 copies in the first seven days, 100,000 before midsummer, and 300,000 before the end of the year. So high was the demand that it kept three paper mills at work, and three power presses running twenty-four hours a day. Overseas sales were astronomical; more than a million and a half copies flew off the shelves in England, and the book was translated into sixteen languages by the time the American Civil War broke out in 1861. Eliza's story did much to convince Northerners that Southern slavery had to end. It is said that President Lincoln greeted Harriet Beecher Stowe during the American Civil War with the words "So this is the little lady who started this great big war."

The products based on Harriet Beecher Stowe's novel were endless. You could eat off *Uncle Tom's Cabin* dishes, sing *Uncle Tom's Cabin* songs, go to *Uncle Tom's Cabin* plays, and even put together this *Uncle Tom's Cabin* jigsaw puzzle.

Escaping from slavery took daring and cleverness, but Henry "Box" Brown's plan was perhaps the most ingenious of all. In 1851, with the help of a storekeeper in Richmond, Virginia, Brown had himself shipped in a crate to friends in Philadelphia. Tossed from wagon to baggage cart to steamer, sometimes upside down, he survived and arrived, he later wrote, "a free-man, but . . . too weak, by reason of long confinement in that box, to be able to stand, so immediately swooned away."

French sitting in Lucie's cell in Lucie's clothes! Meanwhile, Lucie had escaped.

Safely across the border, the Blackburns were reunited. They moved to Toronto, where they established the city's first cab service and helped other fugitive slaves settle. For her part in Lucie's escape, Mrs. Lightfoot was fined twenty-five dollars, and Mrs. French moved to Upper Canada to avoid trouble with the law.

The Underground Railroad

Many slaves who found their way to Canada did so with the help of the "Underground Railroad." There was no actual railroad; it was a secret network of brave people, both black and white. Those who helped fugitives were called "conductors," the routes were "rails," safe houses where runaways could hide along the way were "stations," and the runaways were "cargo" or "freight." Some conductors were members of organized groups, but others, mostly black, simply helped runaways who turned up. Slaves were more likely to trust a black stranger not to betray them.

One black conductor was John Parker, a foundry owner from Ripley, Ohio, who rowed runaways from Kentucky across the Ohio River. One of Parker's white employees was the son of a Kentucky plantation owner, and he challenged Parker to free any of his father's slaves. Parker took the dare and made his way to the slave quarters, where he met a couple who wanted to flee. It would not be easy; the master kept a lit candle and a loaded pistol beside him, and the slaves' child slept at the foot of his bed. Parker crept into the master's bedroom, grabbed the baby, deliberately knocked over the candle and pistol, and ran. When the escapees were halfway across the river they heard gunshots, but they made it across and safely into the hands of another conductor before their master arrived in Ohio.

Levi and Catharine Coffin were white conductors in Newport, Indiana, who helped an estimated three thousand slaves to freedom. In his *Reminiscences*, Coffin recalls how the traffic through his station grew over time:

> In the winter of 1826–27, fugitives began to come to our house, and as it became more widely known on different routes that the slaves fleeing from bondage would find a welcome and shelter at our house, and be forwarded safely on their journey, the number increased.... I found it necessary to keep a team and a wagon always at command, to convey the fugitive slaves on their journey.... These journeys had to be made at night, often through deep mud and bad roads.... Every precaution to evade pursuit had to be used, as the hunters were often on the track, and sometimes ahead of the slaves.

Harriet Tubman

One conductor became known as the "Moses of her people" because, like Moses in the Bible, she guided so many slaves to freedom. When she heard that she was about to be sold, Harriet Tubman escaped slavery in Maryland in 1849. A sympathetic white woman directed her to a safe house and gave her the names of two other people who would help her. Runaways, who rarely had maps and usually

Harriet Tubman was so notorious among slave owners for successfully escorting slaves to freedom – she freed over three hundred – that there was a $40,000 reward for her capture. "I never ran my train off the track," she proudly told an interviewer, "and I never lost a passenger."

couldn't read signposts, fled under cover of darkness. They counted on the North Star to steer them in the right direction. Using it as her guide, Tubman arrived at last in Philadelphia.

Again and again she returned south, making a total of nineteen trips by 1860. Tubman would try to leave on a Saturday night, knowing that owners couldn't advertise in the newspapers for any missing slaves until Monday. She even managed to lead a group of eleven people, including her brother and his wife, from Maryland to Canada. She found clever ways to conceal her identity. Once, disguised as a frail old woman, she heard some men reading her "wanted" poster, which said she was illiterate. She quickly buried her nose in a book.

During the Civil War, Tubman worked for the North as a cook, nurse, and guide, and she was the first woman to lead a raid, liberating more than seven hundred slaves along a river in South Carolina. To encourage them to escape, she stood on the deck of a gunboat singing, "Come along! Come along! Don't be alarmed / Uncle Sam is rich enough to give you all a farm."

The Dred Scott Case

Dred Scott was a slave in St. Louis, Missouri, when his owner took him to the free state of Illinois and then to Wisconsin, a free territory, before they returned to Missouri. While they were in Wisconsin, Scott met and married Harriet Robinson, who became the property of Scott's owner. When the owner died in 1843, Scott and Harriet became the widow's slaves. Three years later, the Scotts went to court to win their freedom. Lawyers for the Scotts argued that they were free because they had lived on free land. The St. Louis circuit court agreed with them, but their owner appealed the decision. In 1857, the U.S. Supreme Court heard Dred Scott's case and ruled against him in a 7–2 decision that many legal experts today consider one of the high court's worst judgments.

Chief Justice Roger B. Taney, a Southern slaveholder, based his decision on racism. Because Scott was black, Taney said, he was not a citizen and had no right to sue. Blacks were "beings of an inferior order . . . so far inferior that they had no rights which the white man was bound to respect." Scott was property, every citizen had a right to transport property, and that included slaves. Taney also said that Congress could not pass laws to keep slavery out of free territories like Wisconsin. The decision caused joy in the South and fury in the North.

The Battle Begins

Tensions between North and South were growing. In 1854, Congress passed the Kansas–Nebraska Act, which let the people who had settled those two territories (not yet states) decide by vote whether the lands would be slave or free. That law provoked armed skirmishes in Kansas between free-soilers, who opposed slavery and had moved to Kansas from the North, and Southerners, who had settled there with their slaves. On the antislavery side was the gray-bearded abolitionist John Brown, a deeply religious man who believed the Bible called on him to take bold action against the sin of American slavery. With his five sons, he freed some slaves, but also gained a reputation for brutality after executing five proslavery settlers. The fighting in Kansas did not resolve the slavery question, and Brown spent the next few years traveling the country to convince supporters that only a violent uprising could end slavery.

The target he chose to begin the battle was the federal armory in Harpers Ferry, Virginia (now in West Virginia), where weapons and ammunition were stored. His plan was to steal the weapons, free and arm slaves, march toward the mountains, and ignite a general slave revolt that he thought would spread throughout the country.

On the night of October 16, 1859, Brown and a band of twelve white and five black men, armed with a rifle and two pistols each, crossed the railroad bridge leading to the armory. The raiders holed up in the armory overnight, but locals soon discovered them and sounded the alarm. Federal troops arrived to find a drunken mob besieging the raiders. Two of Brown's sons were dead, five of his men had escaped, others were wounded, and seven were taken prisoner, including Brown.

Two of the blacks in the raid were tried and executed. One of them, John Anthony Copeland, wrote to his parents from his jail cell, asking them to "remember that it was a 'Holy Cause,' . . . remember that if I must die I die in trying to liberate a few of my poor and oppressed people from my condition of servitude."

Brown faced trial on the charge of treason against the State of Virginia, and against the advice of his attorney he refused to defend himself on the grounds of insanity. He believed that he had waged a "holy war," and that his hanging would further the crusade against slavery.

Although anti-violence abolitionists did not wholeheartedly support Brown, they considered him a martyr. Garrison's *Liberator* labeled the raid "misguided, wild, and apparently insane," but even Garrison praised Brown: "I am prepared to say, 'Success to every slave insurrection at the South,'" and "I see in every slave on the Southern plantation a *living John Brown*." Blacks embraced John Brown as a hero. On the day of his execution, three thousand gathered in Boston in his honor, and in Detroit the Brown Liberty Singers sang "Ode to Old Capt. John Brown."

Brown himself had predicted that his death would not spell victory for his executioners. Before his hanging, he wrote, "The crimes of this guilty land will never be purged away; but with Blood."

A New President

In 1860, candidates for the nation's highest office battled over the issue of slavery for months. Abraham Lincoln, the Republican candidate, had spoken out against slavery years earlier, saying that it violated a leading principle of the Declaration of Independence. But he knew that he would not be elected president if he called for an end to slavery. Instead, he just opposed expanding slavery beyond the boundaries of the current slave states.

Lincoln won the election, and on March 4, 1861, he was sworn in as president of the United States. By then, seven Southern states had already withdrawn from the country and formed the Confederate States of America. Their constitution protected slaveholders' rights and emphasized that slaveholders could move slaves to any states or territories. Four more states would later join the Confederacy.

Lincoln considered himself to be president of the entire country, slave states and free. In his inaugural address, he said he had no intention of interfering "with the institution of slavery in the States where it exists." His primary goal was to hold the country together.

Southerners didn't trust Lincoln. Six weeks later, on April 12, 1861, Confederate forces fired on the federal Fort Sumter in Charleston Harbor, and the Civil War began.

John Brown's raid on the Harpers Ferry armory terrified Southerners, who feared that the abolitionists were planning to invade the South. This print shows Brown holding hostages inside the fire-engine house, just before the gate was broken down and Brown was captured.

Blacks in the American Civil War

As they had in the War of Independence and the War of 1812, blacks joined the fight. They knew that if Confederate (Rebel) forces caught them they faced punishment, and that freed blacks among them might be re-enslaved, yet they were willing to take that risk.

The slave Robert Smalls was pilot of a steam-powered vessel, the *Planter*, in Charleston Harbor. The ship served as a cotton boat in peacetime, but during the war the South put it to work as a gunboat. On May 12, 1862, the *Planter* was loaded with weapons for two Rebel forts. That night, after the white crew members went home, Smalls and the other slaves cleaned the ship, as usual. Their families often brought dinner to them on board, so the deck patrol asked no questions when they arrived. Around three in the morning, Smalls gave the order for the ship to leave port, and slowly it steamed into the harbor. The Confederate flag was flying, and the ship sounded the correct signal – two long pulls and a jerk at the whistle cord – as it moved past Fort Sumter. But as the *Planter* approached the Northern (Union) blockade, the crew pulled down the Rebel colors and raised a white flag, a sign of surrender. Smalls and his crew not only delivered a valuable vessel with heavy weaponry to the Union, but knowledge of Confederate

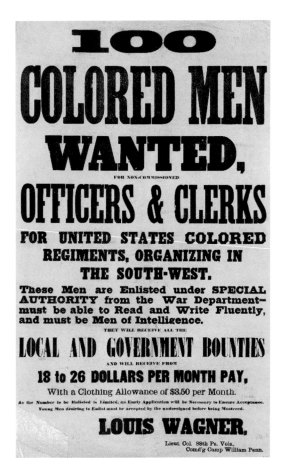

100 COLORED MEN WANTED,

FOR NON-COMMISSIONED

OFFICERS & CLERKS

FOR UNITED STATES COLORED REGIMENTS, ORGANIZING IN THE SOUTH-WEST.

These Men are Enlisted under SPECIAL AUTHORITY from the War Department—must be able to Read and Write Fluently, and must be Men of Intelligence.

THEY WILL RECEIVE ALL THE

LOCAL AND GOVERNMENT BOUNTIES

AND WILL RECEIVE FROM

18 to 26 DOLLARS PER MONTH PAY,

With a Clothing Allowance of $3.50 per Month.

As the Number to be Enlisted is Limited, an Early Application will be Necessary to Ensure Acceptance. Young Men desiring to Enlist must be accepted by the undersigned before being Mustered.

LOUIS WAGNER,

Lieut. Col. 88th Pa. Vols.,
Comd'g Camp William Penn.

In 1862, Congress finally authorized the Union army to recruit black soldiers. The War Department promised they would be treated the same as whites, but the promise was not kept.

defenses and waterways. He went on to enlist in the U.S. Navy and become a captain.

Smalls was far from the only slave who faced danger for the Union cause. William A. Jackson was a house servant and coachman for Jefferson Davis, the president of the Confederacy. Whites had the habit of speaking freely in front of their slaves, assuming they would not understand what was said. Jackson did. On May 3, 1862, he crossed into Union lines near Fredericksburg, Virginia, to report a discussion Davis had had with his military leadership. The information was important enough that the Union general immediately telegraphed it to the War Department. No one today knows the details, but one officer credited "Jeff Davis' coachman" in a letter he sent to the Secretary of War. Even Confederate General Robert E. Lee wrote, "The chief source of information to the enemy is through our negroes."

Since the start of the war, blacks had served in the U.S. Navy, but Lincoln hesitated to enlist black foot soldiers into the Union army. He was afraid that if he did so, he would anger border states like Maryland, which still allowed slavery but remained loyal to the Union. This changed in July 1862. The Union army was taking a beating, and Congress realized that it needed black soldiers.

Free at Last

On September 22, 1862, Lincoln announced that on the first day of the next year he would issue a proclamation to free all the slaves in the Rebel states. January 1 was traditionally the day when slaves were sold, but on New Year's Day in 1863, Lincoln's Emancipation Proclamation immediately freed thousands.

Anna Woods, a slave in Texas, remembered that soldiers came to the fields one Monday morning to tell the slaves the news. "They come a-shouting," she said. "I remember one woman. She jumped on a barrel and she shouted. She jumped off and she shouted. . . . She jumped back on again and shouted some more. She kept that up for a long time, just jumping on a barrel and back off again."

Early in the war, Frederick Douglass had been outraged with Lincoln when the president refused to make freeing the slaves the goal of the war. But in 1863, after Lincoln issued the Emancipation Proclamation and authorized black enlistment, Douglass and Lincoln met. Douglass saw in Lincoln "a deeper moral conviction against slavery than I had ever seen before in anything spoken or written by him."

Lincoln took another big step toward advancing freedom on November 19,

1863, when he spoke on the battlefield in Gettysburg, Pennsylvania. The event was to honor soldiers who had died four months earlier in the bloodiest battle of the Civil War. Lincoln spoke for just three minutes, but his short speech changed the idea of the war from one of preserving the Union to one of freedom for all people.

Lincoln began by saying, "Four score and seven years ago, our fathers brought forth on this continent, a new nation conceived in Liberty and dedicated to the proposition that all men are created equal." He used the Founders' words about equality in a way that the Founders had not. He used them to call for freedom for *all* people, and said equality was the ideal for which the men on the battlefield "gave their last full measure of devotion." After that, people in the North and in the South, both blacks and whites, viewed the war as a battle over slavery.

On April 9, 1865, the Civil War ended in victory for the North. Days later, on April 14, Lincoln was assassinated by an actor, John Wilkes Booth, in revenge for the South's defeat. A few months later, Douglass received a parcel in the mail. It was from Lincoln's widow, Mary Todd Lincoln, and contained Lincoln's "favorite walking staff." She was distributing mementos to people she knew her husband had honored, and Douglass, whom he had called "my friend Douglass" at his second inaugural reception, was one of these. Thanking the First Lady, Frederick Douglass wrote that "this inestimable memento of his Excellency will be retained in my possession while I live – an object of sacred interest . . . as an indication of his humane interest in the welfare of my whole race."

Douglass later wrote that Lincoln "was one of the very few Americans, who could entertain a Negro and converse with him without in anywise reminding him of the unpopularity of his color." He was, said Douglass, "the black man's President: the first to show any respect for their rights as men."

The official end to slavery came on December 6, 1865, when Congress put into law the Thirteenth Amendment to the Constitution. It prohibits slavery and involuntary servitude except as punishment for a crime.

After the War

The end of the war did not end prejudice against blacks or bring prosperity to the former slaves or their descendants. Well into the 1940s, laws in the South that prohibited "loitering" (standing around or walking slowly) allowed white law officers to arrest and charge blacks for trivial reasons. When they could not pay the fines, the courts sent them to work for whites as forced laborers on roads, in coal mines, in lumber camps, and on plantations. Many of them died without being able to get word to their families.

The army did not fully integrate until after World War II, and it took a persistent civil rights movement in the 1950s and 1960s to eliminate the obstacles that black Americans faced in education, employment, housing, and voting. Improvements came with the passage of the Civil Rights Act of 1964 and the Voting Rights Act of 1965. Many Americans were skeptical in 2007, when Barack Obama, a black man, announced his candidacy for the presidency. But on November 4, 2008, he was elected president of the United States.

CHAPTER 11
BLACKBIRDERS, COOLIES, AND SLAVE GIRLS: ASIA AND THE SOUTHERN PACIFIC

The region of Asia and the Southern Pacific encompasses a vast area with people of many religions, cultures, and histories. Over land and by sea, slaves have been captured, ransomed, and traded, and over time, various patterns of slavery have developed.

India

Buddhism and Hinduism are ancient religions with followers all over the world. They are rooted in India, where slavery was a part of life for people of both faiths for thousands of years.

Buddha, who founded Buddhism in the sixth to fifth centuries BCE, taught that being a slave was one of the most painful miseries a person could experience. He cautioned his followers not to live off money earned in the slave trade, and told them to treat their slaves humanely, assign them work they could manage, give them an occasional holiday, feed them, pay them, and care for them when they were ill. The reward for this would be loyal workers. But his teachings did not question the idea of slavery.

Early Buddhist writings offer a glimpse of the lives of slaves, often a grim mixture of ill treatment, long hours, and hard work. One story describes the life of Punika, a slave girl who fetched water from the break of dawn until nightfall, even in the freezing winter months. Though her master was a devout Buddhist, he did nothing to lighten her burden. In another tale, Rajjumala's mistress liked to catch hold of the girl's hair as a convenient handle when she wanted to slap or kick her. In self-defense, the slave had someone shave her head. That made her mistress so angry that she tied a rope around the girl's head and beat her savagely. The slave managed to escape, but in such despair that she tried to take her own life.

In the sacred book Dialogues of the Buddha, a slave compares himself with a king:

He is a man and so am I. But the king lives in the full enjoyment of the five pleasures of the senses – a very god methinks – and here am I a slave, working for him, rising before him and retiring later to rest, keen to carry out his pleasure, anxious to make myself agreeable in deed and word, watching his very looks.

Life as a slave among Hindus was not much different. Kali, a slave in a Hindu household, thought her mistress did not deserve her reputation for having a gentle temper. She asked herself, "Now, does my mistress have an inward ill temper that she does not show because I do my work so carefully?" She set out to test her. Three mornings in a row, Kali slept late. Her mistress's patience began to fray. She called Kali a "wicked slave," scowled, and on the third morning challenged the girl – "Well now, Kali, why did you get up late today?"

"That's nothing, mistress," replied Kali carelessly.

Angered by her slave's sauciness, her mistress grabbed a doorbolt and hit Kali on the head. Kali marched off, exposing her bloodied head – and her mistress's ill temper – to the neighbors.

In India there were degrees of slavery. People in debt bondage sold themselves to a landowner who settled their debts, like back taxes or fines, in exchange for their labor. Those in debt bondage could not be punished physically, and the women could not be abused sexually. Not so, permanent slaves. They were of a lower rank, and were assigned "impure" work like handling leftover food, animal dung, or corpses.

Even though Hindu and Buddhist religious scriptures told people not to buy and sell human beings, slaves from local tribal groups worked on large estates in the fertile river valleys of southern India and were traded from ports along the Malabar Coast, India's western shore. This slave trade persisted well into modern times.

Islamic armies invaded India in the eighth century CE, bringing with them African slaves, mostly from Ethiopia, as well as a new religion. Muslim rulers continued to import Africans for centuries, prizing them as soldiers and excellent sailors who protected ships against pirates on the Indian Ocean. Freed Africans even established kingdoms in western India, and could rise to positions of high authority.

From the thirteenth century on, slaves were traded inside India, and slavery continued there well into the nineteenth century, when the British were the co-lonial power. The British tried to curb the slave trade, which had been illegal in

Britain's West Indian colonies since 1808. In 1843, they passed a law that appeared to make slavery illegal, but it was not publicized. Permanent slavery diminished, but debt bondage persists in India even today.

Southeast Asia

From the sixteenth century on, Western nations fought to control Southeast Asia – the area from the south of China to the north of Australia, and as far east as New Guinea, including parts of the Chinese mainland and many island nations. Spain maintained control of the Philippines until 1898. The Dutch and British fought over parts of what is today Indonesia for many years, but by 1824, Indonesia belonged to the Dutch. The British claimed Singapore in 1819, and in 1842 a treaty gave Britain control over Hong Kong, which it held until 1997, when the territory was returned to China.

Whether people owned debt slaves or chattel slaves, the relationship between slave and owner was usually closer in Southeast Asia than in the Americas. Slaves could earn money by hiring themselves out, and their children could hope for a chance to move up the social ladder. Still, slaves remained slaves with no control over their lives; there was always the worry that they would be given away as gifts, sold, or passed on to the owner's children.

Slaves did a wide range of jobs. They were potters, scribes, soldiers, sailors, messengers, traders, or interpreters. Both men and women cleaned and cooked in their owners' homes, or planted and harvested rice. Women were especially valued as concubines, and as dancers and singers.

Enter Islam

Islam became established in Southeast Asia around 1400. Because Muslims could not legally enslave other Muslims, slave traders traveled inland or by ship to capture non-Muslims in order to satisfy the demand for workers.

In the Malay Peninsula (today's Malaysia), the people living on the coast commonly raided the Orang Asli, Malay for "original peoples," who lived in the foothills or mountains or along inland rivers. A century-old account describes how the coastal Malays carried out their raids:

> He would build himself a small shelter, and never leave it until he had discovered . . . where they [the Orang Asli] usually spent the night. Accompanied by a few accomplices, he would then repair to the spot at nightfall, and the party, concealing themselves until dark, would wait . . . until the "hill-men" were asleep. The Malays would then fire several rifle shots, spreading terror and confusion in every family, whose breaking up made them an easy prey to their assailants, who would promptly make a rush for the spot where they heard the shrieks of the women and children. The girls were, as a rule, at once knocked on the head, and the boys were carried off and sold as slaves.

Boys were the preferred prey, but women and girls were also sold as slaves. The adult men were usually killed. Some Orang Asli cooperated with the Malays, kidnapping children to sell them. The standard price? Two rolls of coarse cloth, a hatchet, a chopper, and an iron cooking pot.

The Dutch Arrive

In the early 1600s, when the Dutch colonized Southeast Asia, they set up the Dutch East India Company to trade in rice, salt, precious woods, silks, porcelain, pepper, nutmeg – and human beings. They opened a trading post in Jakarta, which they called Batavia, and by the eighteenth century they had control of all of Java. The Javanese had owned slaves whom they considered to be a part of their families. Not so the Dutch slave owners, so their slaves felt less loyal and were more likely to run away.

Christina was the slave of a Dutch East India Company merchant, Abraham Walburg, and his wife, Sara, in 1776. Christina wanted to live with her boyfriend, Samuel Brandt, and under traditional Southeast Asian customs she probably could have arranged this. She tried to bargain for her freedom, telling the Walburgs that Samuel was willing to buy her. To win them over, she introduced them to Samuel. Sara hired him to repair two silver dog collars, a gold flower hairpin, diamond earrings, and even gold buttons belonging to another slave, but Samuel could not convince the Walburgs to sell Christina. Even when he offered to rent her and teach her how to embroider and make bridal veils – a skill that would make her a valuable money-earner for the Walburgs – they refused.

Finally, Christina escaped. Her mistress sent her slaves to Samuel's house and he pretended to look for her, but in time Samuel too ran off. For nineteen months the couple lived secretly in a hut next to his brother's house. Samuel closed off the door to hide Christina, who ventured out rarely, and only at night. But then a suspicious neighbor tipped off the authorities, who raided the house. We have no record of the punishment meted out to Christina and Samuel, but in another case of runaways the man was sentenced to a flogging with a cat-o'-nine-tails, branding, and twenty-five years of hard labor, and the woman to a beating and a year of serving her master in chains. Did Christina and Samuel suffer the same fate?

The Malay Maritime World

Not all Dutch were slave owners. Some became slaves themselves. C. Z. Pieters was captain of the Dutch ship *Petronella*, which was sailing through the Celebes Sea in June 1838 when another ship approached. Pieters shouted to its crew but no one answered. He called again, but there was still no reply as the vessel pulled

A BRIDE AND HER FIFTY-NINE SLAVES

Life in the colonies must have seemed luxurious to the Dutch colonists. One couple had fifty-nine servants to wait on them – several young men and maids to accompany them when they left the house, a slave at the entrance to run errands, and slaves to groom the horses, cook, work in the dairy, do the sewing, and tend the garden. They had slaves to stand behind their chairs at meals, and a slave orchestra to entertain them on the harp, viol, and bassoon as they ate.

nearer the *Petronella*. A final time Pieters called out. This time the ship came so close that he could see that Balangingi pirates were pursuing him. The Balangingi, from the Sulu Archipelago, were in the business of slave raiding.

The pirate ship fired its cannon and flashed a light, signaling other ships to approach. Soon, ten boats surrounded the *Petronella*, and they followed the Dutch ship all night. In the morning the pirates fired more shots, killing two crewmen and badly injuring two others. Captain Pieters was carried off into slavery.

Piracy was big business on the Sulu and Celebes Seas, where the Philippines are today. Slave trading already existed there, but it became a booming business as the need for laborers grew. Everyone in the west wanted tea from China, but all they had to offer in exchange was silver, which was expensive. If European and American merchants could get less expensive products like mother-of-pearl, cinnamon, and birds' nests (for soup-making) from the Sulu Islands, they could trade them to the Chinese for tea. The problem was that the Europeans and Americans needed workers to harvest the precious resources. From the late eighteenth century to the mid-nineteenth century, two groups of people – the Balangingi and Iranun – would stop at nothing to provide those workers. They raided the waterways and coastal settlements of today's Philippines, Indonesia, and Malaysia for people and for the contents of their ships.

The voyage to Sulu sometimes took months. The captives were fed little, bound with strips of rattan, and often forced to work on board the ship, as one reported:

> They sat there . . . on the deck of the boat under the scorching heat of the sun, the rain, and in the wind's eye. Some simply collapsed over their oar, dying. Others were untied just on the verge of passing out, in order to regain consciousness, only to be tied up once again to the oar.

The Balangingi sometimes forced captives to go with them on their raids. Francisco Thomas was just twelve years old when the Balangingi killed his brother and father and captured him. Weeks later, they made him take the oars of a slave-raiding ship, a *garay*. In the boat was the very man who had killed his father.

Raiders traded slaves all along the Sulu Archipelago and even as far away as Borneo, where some of the most unfortunate became victims of human sacrifice.

Slaves who arrived in Sulu usually did unskilled work on farms and in forests, fisheries, and salt fields. Educated captives were put to work as bureaucrats, scribes, translators, or tutors, as slave owners wanted to take advantage of their skills. Pieters, the captain of the *Petronella*, was spared heavy labor because he had some knowledge of medicine:

> One day my master and his wife asked me to what kind of work I was accustomed. I said that I could not work and that my former master had only employed me in looking after his goods, accounts and dollars, and giving medicine to sick people. When they learnt this from me, my master went and told everyone that he had a slave who could cure all kinds of sickness.

People were eager for Pieters's help. He asked to be paid in rice and sweet potatoes, which he shared with other captives. One woman promised him two slaves

The *garay* was a broad, swift-moving slave-raiding vessel that carried as many as a hundred people. With an enormous sail and sixty oars in two rows, the boat could travel over water at speeds better than ten knots, or about eleven miles per hour (18 kph).

This well-armed Iranun pirate wears a vest of red quilted cotton, and carries a dagger, a spear, and a sword decorated with human hair.

and freedom if he could cure her husband. The man recovered but he did not keep his wife's promise.

A small number of slaves became wealthy, and eventually free, as rewards for good service. Some compared their lives to what they had had before and felt they were no worse off. A Malay man who was selling coconuts told one traveler that he was a captive and had no wish to change:

> I enquired why he did not profit by the opportunity to escape and revisit his country. "Why should I?" he replied, "there is something to regret everywhere; here I am well enough, my master treats me as if I were one of his kindred, I am well paid, and could save money if I wished; in my own country I know I could not do better, and perhaps should not fare as well; therefore, I prefer remaining here."

Nevertheless, being a slave meant you could be sold over and over again, and abused at the hands of cruel owners. Small wonder that slaves risked death to escape. They fled in canoes to foreign ships, where sailors gave them asylum, or they found refuge on neighboring islands, or a friend or family member paid ransom for them. European ship captains often paid for captives, who worked off the price as crew members.

Captain Pieters was desperate to escape. He met a friendly woman on board a trading vessel and gave her a letter for other ship captains that explained his situation. While he waited for a reply, he got his owner to agree to sell him. His owner didn't know about the letter, but he wanted to make a profit, so he tried to sell Pieters to the very captain who had received the letter! The sale almost fell through. The price for Pieters was a thousand dollars, so high that the captain had to say no. Pieters had to find a way to get the price lowered so he decided to pretend to be ill, and refused all food. "I felt really indisposed on the third day, which I was not sorry for," he said, "as I thought it was better to die than to live at the mercy of people who could do with me as they pleased." The next morning, he learned that the captain had purchased him for the bargain price of three hundred dollars.

From 1770 to 1870, the Iranun and Balangingi captured as many as 300,000 people. By the 1870s, however, the Spanish navy was sailing those waters, and it was too strong a force for the Sulu. Their slave trade ended.

But neither piracy nor slavery was over for good. By the 1970s, pirates and other criminals were reappearing on those seas, which were busy with fishing vessels, boats filled with refugees from Indochina, and tankers and other commercial vessels. Today, raiders are still seizing ships and capturing innocent people.

In the islands of the Southern Pacific, slavery existed long before the Europeans arrived. Captives of war were enslaved in Tahiti. In what is now New Zealand, when the Maori were victorious in battle, they enslaved the losers, sacrificing some of them and eating others. In Hawaii the slaves were a separate class known as the *kauwā*. They lived apart from other people and were often distinguished from them by a tattoo on their foreheads.

Blackbirding

After the Europeans arrived, the market for slaves changed. The island of Fiji needed workers for its sugar and cotton plantations, and the Australian adventurer and doctor James Patrick Murray wanted money. He bought a ship, the *Carl*, in 1871 and traveled to the islands of New Hebrides (now Vanuatu). As islanders approached the ship in their canoes, the crew lured them closer by showing off beads and pipes and other temptations. But Murray had no interest in buying and selling trinkets. He wanted men. His crew quickly threw iron weights onto the canoes, forcing them to overturn or sink and making it easy for the sailors to grab the astonished passengers.

Willing or not, the people of New Hebrides would become laborers in Fiji. One night, these reluctant passengers rebelled. The *Carl*'s ruthless crew used guns and daggers against them and threw the wounded captives into the sea, killing more than seventy. Only twenty men survived, and the crew sold them in Fiji.

Murray was a blackbirder, someone who kidnapped Pacific islanders and transported them to Fiji, Australia, Hawaii, and other lands to work. Some blackbirders enticed their prey with false promises of jobs, but the name "blackbirders" came from one of their nastiest tactics: they left their ships late at night, dressed all in black, so the islanders would not see them before they were whisked away.

In the mid-1800s, when blackbirding was most common, the raiders targeted villages along the coast. They took the youngest and healthiest men, leaving the others behind to try to survive without their strongest workers.

COOLIES: SLAVES BY ANY OTHER NAME?

Two young men left New Bedford, Massachusetts, on a whaling ship around 1850. When they wrote about their adventures, they described seeing slave traders from Peru taking Chinese workers to a miserable life in the mines in South America. They wrote that the Chinese were promised well-paying jobs in a rich country. Instead:

As soon as they get them on shipboard, a guard is stationed over them, with orders to shoot down the first one that shows any signs of resistance. Being kept such close prisoners, and on the coarsest food, they are naturally joyous at the sight of land, and leave the vessel with glad hearts, only to enter the slavery of the Peruvian mines. This species of slave-trade is, like the African slave-trade in our own land, forbidden by the laws of the country, but secretly connived and winked at.

These Chinese workers were known as coolies, a word that, in written Chinese, meant "bitter labor." It was a perfect description of their lot.

Most coolies were transported to Latin America between the 1840s and the 1870s, when the Atlantic slave trade had ended and cheap labor was scarce. Although some were kidnapped, many

The Australian territory of Queensland depended on people of the South Pacific to work on its sugar plantations, and actively recruited them in the 1860s. Demand remained high in 1895, when this photo was taken, and laws were in effect to end blackbirding.

Blackbirding Trials

The British government was sensitive to charges that seamen on British ships were capturing natives. They sent George Palmer, the captain of the *Rosario*, to investigate. In 1869 he was patrolling the seas when he saw the ship *Daphne* headed for Fiji. Palmer had served in West Africa, and he knew how to recognize a slave ship. The *Daphne* made him suspicious. The *Rosario* intercepted the ship, which was supposed to carry only fifty-eight passengers but had more than one hundred people from New Hebrides on board. "They were stark naked,"

Palmer said, "and had not even a mat to lie upon; the shelves were just the same as might be knocked up for a lot of pigs, – no bunks or partitions of any sort being fitted."

Palmer brought the ship's American skipper and Australian owner to the Sydney Water Police Court but failed to convince the judges to try them for piracy. The judges claimed that there was not enough evidence to show that the people had been taken against their will. Next, Palmer tried to have the *Daphne* condemned as a slave ship, but the judge ruled that the law against the slave trade didn't apply in the South Pacific. Palmer later wrote a book, *Kidnapping in the South Seas*, which opened people's eyes to the outrages of blackbirding.

In Fiji, the trial of a man named Kapitani also stirred public sentiment. Kapitani had been kidnapped by an American, Achilles Underwood, who had forced him to work long hours, flogged him, and "struck him with a hot iron, searing and burning into his skin." He had even locked Kapitani and others into a small shack where they couldn't lie down, and where they were given water only twice a day. After four days Kapitani escaped, grabbed an ax, and killed Underwood.

Nobody at the trial had much sympathy for the dead Underwood. Even his wife said she had warned her husband that the laborers "would retaliate upon him for his cruelty to them." Kapitani was found guilty of manslaughter, a lesser crime than murder. He was sentenced to one year of hard labor, but released after only a few months.

By the time Kapitani killed Underwood in 1871, public opinion was turning against blackbirding. Bishop J.C. Patteson had been an outspoken critic of the trade, but his face was not well-known to Pacific islanders. On September 20 of that year, natives of the Solomon Islands killed him and another missionary in revenge for the way white men treated the islanders. Their deaths horrified British citizens in New Zealand, and the news reports brought attention to the kidnapping of natives. New Zealand's premier, William Fox, called blackbirding an "infamous slave trade," and in 1872, Britain passed the Pacific Islanders' Protection Act, making it illegal for any British subject to kidnap a native. In 1875, Fiji became a British territory. Britain now policed a huge swath of the Pacific Ocean. Slowly, blackbirding came to an end.

were tricked into signing on. Desperate to escape poverty, war, and famine, they left southern Chinese ports to work in sugar plantations or mines. Unlike African slaves, they earned some pay, though far less than local workers. Conditions on the ocean crossing, known as the "Pacific Passage," were at least as dreadful as on the Middle Passage across the Atlantic. In the 1850s about 40 percent of the Chinese died on the way to Peru. Although the coolies were technically not slaves because they came with contracts for five to eight years of labor, many didn't survive that long. Because of their wretched treatment on Cuban sugar plantations, for example, 75 percent died before their contracts expired. Word got back to China, and with the Chinese government's intervention, the coolie trade was abolished in 1874.

China

Slavery was ending in the South Pacific, but it continued in China. Ancient Chinese writings tell us that slaves played a role there from the earliest times. A slave was considered to be a different sort of person – a creature of lower status (*chien*, "not good," unlike ordinary people who were *liang*, "good"). This lowly status was passed on to the slave's children. To make sure that everyone recognized people who were *chien*, slaves were often tattooed or mutilated, their noses cut off.

Sometimes the government would enslave a whole family. If a family member was found guilty of being a traitor, the traitor would be executed, along with his hapless male relatives. The traitor's female relatives and children would become slaves. But most people became slaves by the tragic routes of war and poverty.

A Chinese philosopher who lived over two thousand years ago described how war captives became slaves:

> The great state marshals its armies of boats and chariots to attack a blameless country. . . . The people who resist are beheaded, those who do not resist are put in bonds and brought back. The men are made drivers and grooms [to take care of the horses]. The women are made grinders of corn.

The *Mui-tsai*

In China as in so many other places, famine forced starving people to sell themselves. Many Chinese became tenant farmers who were bound to their landlords for a few years. Some fell into more permanent forms of bondage.

Sometimes families sank so deeply into poverty that they faced a grim choice: either watch their loved ones starve, or sell their children. In China, children of the poor – especially daughters, who were not valued as highly as sons – were often sold into slavery. The consequences for these girls could be disastrous. Called *mui-tsai* ("little younger sister"), they became servants in households both rich and poor. Although the owner was generally expected to arrange a marriage for the girl when she reached her teens, many sold the girls to be concubines or prostitutes.

Janet Lim was born in Hong Kong in 1923. Her father named her Qiu Mei, "Autumn Beauty," after his favorite season. He was unusual for his time and place – a Christian who promised his daughter the rare privilege of an education.

Then bad luck struck. Janet's father died when she was six years old. Her mother could not support her family alone, so she married a man from a nearby town. They sank into poverty, and her mother and stepfather decided to sell eight-year-old Qiu Mei to a dealer. The poor girl was distraught. Her mother promised to come and get her if they could earn the money to buy her back, but this never happened. The child never saw her mother again.

Janet entered the home of a woman who sold children, some as young as four years old. There she had a job she loathed: massaging the fat, lazy woman and serving her tea until she fell asleep. One day the gate was left open, and Janet escaped. She followed the train tracks toward the city where she believed her mother lived, but a passenger on an oncoming train recognized her and returned her to her heartless owner. What happened next was a nightmare.

> I had never seen the mistress so savage before; she was like a tigress, she sprang at me and shouted that I was an ungrateful dog. She got hold of my hair and flung me to the floor. She sat on my stomach and pinched my body between her great long fingernails. They sank deeply into my flesh. . . . I must have fainted, for the next thing I remember is waking up to find myself chained to a door and there I remained chained for a month.

Like the witch who kept Hansel locked up until Gretel outwitted her, Janet's mistress was more cruel than clever. Janet convinced her that she was a medium, someone who could contact the spirits of the dead. Her mistress believed her, and finally released the child from her chains.

A while later, her owner took Janet and some other children to the island of Singapore, which was also under British control. There, an old man and his wife bought her. She and another *mui-tsai* with the same family had no beds to sleep on, and little to eat except leftover rice. Janet did housework and looked after the poultry:

> Indeed the geese were my great friends. I talked to them about my sorrows and worries, and, turning their heads this way and that, they seemed to understand me. . . . I was very lonely, and after my day's work I would go into the garden to be comforted by my friends, the geese.

Mui-tsai were often clothed in rags, like this girl in a 1930 photograph. In China, the custom of selling daughters as *mui-tsai* lasted from ancient times until the Communist Revolution in the 1940s.

But she was terrified of the lecherous old man, who pursued her every night. One night she hid in a treetop. Another night, she hid among the geese – anywhere to escape him. She even thought of taking her life.

Relief finally came when Janet was sent to stay for a time with the mistress's aunt, a "very gentle woman with a soft voice" who shared companionship, food, and even the daily chores with the girl. It was at her house that Janet finally understood what was in store for her: she was to become her elderly master's concubine. The thought horrified her.

When Britain colonized parts of China in the first half of the 1800s, English colonists were disturbed by this sale of girls, and the reports of their miserable lives. Singapore was British soil and, following British law, slavery was illegal there. In the 1920s and 1930s, both the British Parliament and the League of Nations (an early version of the United Nations) labeled the *mui-tsai* practice a form of slavery. That did not stop it, but it was a first step.

It took a law passed by the British colonial government in 1932 to save Janet. All *mui-tsai* were to be registered. When her mistress went to the government office with Janet and the other young *mui-tsai* in her household (dressed up in pretty clothes the girls had never worn before), a "blue-eyed woman" took Janet aside, held her hand, and told her she would be visited regularly and should complain if her mistress mistreated her.

Now that they were protected, the two *mui-tsai* planned their escape. The next morning her friend slipped out to the police to tell her story, and the "blue-eyed lady" came to Janet's house and freed her from slavery.

The disgraced owner had to pay Janet for all her unpaid work. Janet enrolled in a mission school, where she took her English name. She never found her mother, but she got the education her father had promised her, and became a nurse. After World War II she finished her training and became the first Asian head nurse at St. Andrew's Mission Hospital in Singapore. She married an Australian doctor and had three children. In 1958, Janet Lim took another daring step: she told her life story in a book, *Sold for Silver*. Freed *mui-tsai*, like many former slaves, were too ashamed to speak about their past, even among themselves. The *mui-tsai* girls at Janet's school had never sought comfort from each other by sharing their stories. Janet Lim broke the silence, opening a window on a sad chapter of China's history.

The successful battles to end *mui-tsai* service and blackbird-ing were just two strikes against slavery in Asia and the Southern Pacific region. But laws and practice are sometimes two different things, and slavery continues there today.

DEED OF SALE FOR A DAUGHTER, 1927

When Chinese parents gave up their daughters as *mui-tsai*, it was a legal sale. This document outlines the agreement between the parents of ten-year-old Ah-Mui and the person buying her, Chan Yee Koo, in 1927. If Ah-Mui was unhappy and disobeyed her owner, her parents would not be able to buy her back, since the sale of their daughter was final.

This deed of sale is made by Poon Shi of Mak family.

In consequence of urgent need for funds to meet family expenses, I am willing to sell my own daughter, Ah Mui, 10 years of age, born in the afternoon, 23rd day of 11th moon, Mo Ng year (i.e. 25th December, 1918), to Chan Yee Koo through a go-between. In the presence of three parties, it is mutually agreed and arranged that the purchase price is to be 141 dollars. After this sale, Chan Yee Koo shall have the right to change the name of the girl. If the girl is disobedient, Chan Yee Koo shall be allowed to resell her, and the mother shall have no recourse. In the event of any misfortune befallen the girl, there is no blame to either Party. . . .

This is a straightforward sale and purchase between two parties and lest verbal contract is invalid, delivered to Chan Yee Koo as proof thereof.

Poon Shi of Mak Family hereby acknowledges receipt of the purchase price of 141 dollars in full, without deduction.

Finger prints of Poon Shi of Mak Family . . . Go-between, Poon Shi of Chan Family.

Dated
The Republic of China, 13th June, 1927

CHAPTER 12
SLAVERY IS NOT HISTORY: THE MODERN WORLD

When the abolitionists won their battles in Britain and the Americas, they thought that their dreams of a world where every person was free had been realized. Tragically, the fight for freedom isn't over. Millions of people of all ages are enslaved today, leading lives very much like those of slaves hundreds and even thousands of years ago. Some are born into slavery, but others are bought and sold, sometimes for years and sometimes for life. They are paid little or nothing, and have no choice about what work they do, where they live, or what their future holds.

The Aleutian Islands

The United States acquired the Pribilof Islands – St. Paul and St. George, off the southwest coast of Alaska – when it bought Alaska from the Russians in 1867. The islands' fur industry was worth a fortune, but not much of the profit went into the purses of the native Aleut people. After 1910, the government managed the industry. In other words, the Aleuts were government employees whose job it was to slaughter and skin seals and foxes. They had little choice because there was no other place to work. They could work for the government or they could starve.

We take it for granted that government employees get paid in money, and that they have other benefits too. But the Aleuts were not paid in cash, and they certainly didn't receive benefits. Instead, they were given credit at the government store – the only place to buy food – and not only was the food expensive, but the shelves were often nearly empty, so there was hardly anything to buy.

From offices in faraway Washington, D.C., the government controlled the Aleuts' daily lives. They were not allowed to leave the islands without permission. They were not allowed to speak their native language. Their chiefs were not allowed to have any say in how they were governed. Men were even told when they could marry. Until 1924, they were not even allowed U.S. citizenship.

These rules did not always sit well with government officials who worked on the islands and saw the hardship firsthand. In 1910, a government agent wrote to his supervisors in Washington:

[The] fact cannot be denied that the people of St. Paul (and St. George as well) are living in actual slavery and that this condition exists and is maintained under the immediate control and direction of the United States government.

Thirty-one years later, Fredericka Martin, an American nurse on one of the Pribilof Islands, organized a group of whites to try to eat only what the Americans gave the Aleuts.

I planned to limit us to the experiment for a week. One day was enough. Or, rather, too much. We had to calm our surprised, protesting, neglected stomachs before we could go to sleep. It was not only the kind of food but the small quantity which ended our test. I no longer wondered why the kids sneaked around the garbage cans and ate some filthy refuse.

Hard as life was for the Pribilof Aleuts, it was about to get worse. Months after the United States entered World War II in December 1941, the Navy needed the Aleuts' houses, and sent the people to southeastern Alaska, 1,500 miles (2,400 km) away. Their new homes were dilapidated, abandoned fish canneries with poor sanitation, no bunks or mattresses, and only two stoves for 290 people.

When the government sent them back home again, after the war, the natives began to insist on their rights as Americans. One of their supporters was Fredericka Martin. She wrote magazine articles and letters to politicians to raise awareness of the shameful form of slavery imposed on the Aleuts.

In 1951, the Pribilof Aleuts sued the U.S. government for back wages. Alaska became a state in 1959, but the suit was not settled until 1978, when the government's Indian Claims Commission announced that the government would have to pay the Aleuts for the profits made off years of their labor. Sadly, many of the people who had suffered the most were no longer alive to share the wealth.

Freedom eventually came to the Aleuts because they and people like Fredericka Martin exposed the abuses. But totalitarian governments, like the strict Communist regime that used to control Russia, or the Nazi government of Hitler's Germany, punish those who speak out – sometimes by enslaving them.

This Aleutian fisherman is wearing a "gut parka," a lightweight, waterproof jacket made from the guts of a sea lion, harbor seal, fur seal, or whale. The intestines were cleaned, dried, split open, cut into strips, and then sewn together with thread made of fox or whale sinew.

The Soviet Union

The world's first Communist country – the Union of Soviet Socialist Republics, or Soviet Union – established a prison system in the 1930s for anybody who criticized the government. Built by the country's harshest dictator, Josef Stalin, the prison camps, called gulags, were used as a way to stamp out freedom of expression in religion, newspapers, and the arts. The gulags were always in remote areas where the prisoners were forced to do hard physical labor.

Alexander Solzhenitsyn was an artillery officer decorated twice by the Soviet Army for bravery in World War II. But his valor did not help him when he was arrested for writing a letter to a friend criticizing Stalin; he was sentenced to eight years in prison. Following his experience in the gulag, Solzhenitsyn wrote *One Day in the Life of Ivan Denisovich*, which was published after Stalin's death. The novel opened the world's eyes to the brutality of these forced-labor camps in the bitterly cold northern area of Siberia. The workers survived mostly on thin soups with almost no meat or vegetables, a meager daily ration of bread, and mush made from "the amount of oats [Ivan Denisovich] fed to horses when he was a boy, and he never thought he'd long for a handful himself one day!" The cooks cheated the prisoners on their food to feed themselves and buy favors from others. Solzhenitsyn describes the men, wearing leaky boots stuffed with cloth, and rags wrapped around their faces against the icy Siberian wind, as they construct a brick wall, and warm themselves by the stove used to loosen the frozen mortar. Some had been sentenced to ten years, some to twenty-five, but many were not allowed to return home even when they were released from the camps.

Nazi Germany

In World War II, Nazi Germany conquered and occupied most of Europe. As it expanded its army to invade and control more and more land, it had a problem: where would it get workers to farm its fields, produce weapons and ammunition in its factories, and work in its mines? The answer was to enslave the people of the

The Soviet dictator Josef Stalin compelled slave laborers to work on many construction projects, including this canal between the White and Baltic seas.

countries it occupied. The Nazis rounded up Italians, French, Poles, and others, and shipped them to Germany to work. They took men, women, even children as young as six years old, and they didn't care if they tore families apart.

Among the enslaved were three million Russian civilians. Some were sent to work in German homes, where the families were allowed to treat them however they chose. Germany also enslaved Russian prisoners of war, although this was illegal under the Geneva Conventions, treaties that Germany had signed after World War I.

The Nazis' treatment of slave laborers fit their warped ideas about race. They said that Germans were a "superior" race and therefore had the right to enslave and brutalize those who were less than human, like the Slavic people. Signs outside the Krupp factories, which made tanks and munitions, read, "Slavs are slaves," and supervisors did not hesitate to beat workers with whips or clubs for the slightest mistake.

Although the Nazis' ultimate goal was to exterminate groups of people that they felt were inferior, including all Jews, they also exploited Jewish people as slave labor. They rounded up the Jews of Eastern Europe and moved them into crowded and tightly controlled areas known as ghettos. Factories in the Warsaw ghetto in Poland, for example, produced all the uniforms for the German air force. Jews who were not immediately sent to death camps could be assigned to forced-labor camps, where they were often worked to death. In the Hasag plant in Poland, where weapons and explosives were manufactured, the prisoners' skin turned yellow from the chemicals they worked with, and they ultimately died.

China

Sam Lu practiced Falun Gong, a spiritual system the Chinese government banned in 1999, and he was imprisoned for his beliefs. By some estimates, a hundred thousand followers of Falun Gong are now locked up in Chinese forced-labor camps, known as *laogai*.

Sometime after being released from prison, Sam Lu moved to Atlanta, Georgia, where he had been a graduate student in 1996. In the freedom of the United States, he could tell his story without fear. He said he wanted "to let [people] know how some products from China are made and why they are so cheap."

This starved, almost blind Russian prisoner was one of the people liberated by the U.S. Army from Nordhausen, a Nazi slave labor camp, at the end of World War II. At least he was lucky enough to survive.

On June 7, 2000, I was arrested in China only because I handed in a letter at the State Appeal Bureau in Beijing to express my opinion about Falun Gong, which is . . . based on "Truthfulness, Compassion, and Forbearance" and which is being persecuted in China. I was put in a jail in Guangdong Province for almost two months. . . . In prison I was forced to work on export products such as toys and shopping bags without pay. . . . The cell was only about three hundred square feet [28 sq. m.] in size, with twenty prisoners and one toilet inside. They slept and worked in the cell. Sometimes we were forced to work until two a.m. to keep up with the schedule. They only provided two meals a day (only once a week you have meat in your food). In other words, being hungry, you still need to work more than fifteen hours per day. The police used a wire whip to beat you if you did not do a good job or you could not keep up with the schedule.

Lu was also worried about his wife, who had been sentenced to a forced-labor camp for three years for handing out Falun Gong flyers. Her job was to embroider textiles for export. "The hard work, malnutrition and torture made my wife almost lose her eyesight," he said.

Today there are over a thousand *laogai* camps throughout China. The Chinese government imprisons not just Falun Gong practitioners but also Christians and political dissidents – anyone it sees as a threat to its hold on power. The labor camps manufacture products like Christmas lights, stuffed animals, knitted sweaters, and gloves that are sold throughout the world, at low prices, to people who are happy to get a "bargain."

North Korea and Cuba

North Korea and Cuba are also Communist dictatorships that try to stifle anyone who disagrees with them. In one case, a woman was arrested for singing a South Korean pop song in a private home in North Korea. Since South Korea is a free country and North Korea is a totalitarian state, this must have been considered threatening by the authorities; she was imprisoned for her "crime." In North Korea, political prisoners are sent to live in penal labor colonies in remote, mountainous parts of the country, with up to three generations of their families. They are usually given life sentences of forced work in mines, on farms, or in factories.

In Cuba, anti-government activists are assigned to forced labor. Luis Alberto Ferrándiz Alfaro was sentenced to work designing jewelry and furniture for a prison factory for the "crime" of creating anti-government stamps and flyers.

Child Slavery and Children at War

Military groups in some war-torn countries enslave children to work or to fight. If those children survive, the horrors they have experienced often haunt them long after they escape slavery.

Susan was sixteen years old when she was captured by the so-called Lord's Resistance Army in Uganda and made to fight for them. Later, she told the organization Human Rights Watch:

> One boy tried to escape [from the rebels], but he was caught. . . . His hands were tied, and then they made us, the other new captives, kill him with a stick. I felt sick. I knew this boy from before. We were from the same village. I refused to kill him and they told me they would shoot me. They pointed a gun at me, so I had to do it. The boy was asking me, "Why are you doing this?" I said I had no choice. . . . I still dream about the boy from my village who I killed. I see him in my dreams, and he is talking to me and saying I killed him for nothing, and I am crying.

Some children enlist in military groups voluntarily because they see no other way to survive. Ishmael Beah was thirteen when he became a soldier in Sierra Leone. He thought that if he refused, he would be killed by enemy soldiers, or die of starvation. He and the other child soldiers took drugs to escape from the realities of their lives as fighters. Years later, Beah said his soul felt "corrupted" by what he had done. He has written a book about his ordeal, and travels widely to make people aware of the issue of child soldiers.

More than 250,000 children were enslaved in military groups in 2009, according to the United Nations. In Africa, there were 100,000 child soldiers, some as young as seven. Other areas of conflict using children as soldiers include Burma, Chechnya, Colombia, India, Indonesia, Iraq, the Palestinian Territories, Peru, and Sri Lanka.

The United Nations General Assembly took a strong stand against this by unanimously passing the Child Soldiers Protocol on May 25, 2000. This rule prohibits

OUT OF THE WATER AND INTO SCHOOL

Poverty is so severe in Ghana that many parents lease their children to fishermen to raise a little money, sometimes only twenty dollars a year. The children live with a fisherman far from home, and often spend as many as fifteen hours a day on a canoe, doing laborious and sometimes dangerous jobs.

Young children bail water from their boats to keep them afloat. When they are older, they take on the more dangerous task of diving down to untangle fishing nets. Some of them drown.

governments, armies, or other armed groups from recruiting soldiers under the age of eighteen. Unfortunately, the United Nations decree has not stopped the practice.

On Cocoa Farms

Poverty drives some children into backbreaking unpaid labor. Amadou was a young boy when a man promised him a good job in the Ivory Coast (Côte d'Ivoire). The work turned out to be on a plantation growing cocoa and other crops, hundreds of miles from his family in Mali, a poor country in West Africa. There, from the crack of dawn until sundown, Amadou collected cocoa pods and hauled great sacks of them. Flies buzzed around his head, he had to watch for snakes at his feet, and he slept locked in a shack with eighteen other boys, with only a can for a toilet. He was always hungry, and he was beaten if he didn't work quickly enough for the farmer. Some of the boys he worked with died.

Amadou had been a slave for over five years when one boy from his farm managed to escape. He got word to a Malian government official, Abdul Makho, and

Mark Kwadwo was five when his parents sold him to this fisherman. He was rescued by a woman from Missouri who read about him in a newspaper in the United States.

with police help, Makho freed the boys and took them to his home. After they were clean, fed, and clothed, he allowed a British film crew to interview them. That was when Amadou learned that the cocoa beans he harvested made chocolate, a treat he had never tasted. Here is Amadou's message to those who ate that chocolate: "If I had to say something to them, it would not be nice words. They enjoy something I suffered to make; I worked hard for them, but saw no benefit. They are eating my flesh." The film, first broadcast on British television, opened the world's eyes to conditions on many cocoa plantations.

The idea that chocolate Easter bunnies, Santas, and candy bars could depend on slave labor is shocking, and many people think the solution is simple: don't buy chocolate from the Ivory Coast or any other country where slave labor is used to harvest it. But experts in modern slavery tell us that the answer isn't that easy.

Almost half the world's chocolate comes from 600,000 small farms in the Ivory Coast. Some of the farmers employ slaves, but many do not. All the harvested cocoa beans are mixed together when they go to chocolate factories. If we boycott all Ivory Coast chocolate, we hurt the honest farmers who pay their workers. If they lose their farms because no one will buy their chocolate, they and their children will sink into poverty, and perhaps into slavery.

The world's biggest chocolate companies insisted that the child slavery shown in the film was not typical. But two American congressmen, Eliot Engel and Tom Harkin, believed the abuses were common enough that all chocolate products should have a label stating that they were made without slave labor. In 2001, the chocolate companies and congressmen came out with the Cocoa Protocol. It required that the major chocolate companies, antislavery groups, and governments work together to stop the worst forms of child labor and to develop a way to inspect the cocoa plantations. For the first time in history, members of an industry had cooperated to eliminate slavery from their product.

They created the International Cocoa Initiative (ICI), whose programs alert people to the dangers children face on cocoa plantations and train police to spot traffickers. (Traffickers are people who use deceit or coercion to pressure victims into performing work without payment, often in a new location.) The ICI also provides shelters for children rescued from slavery.

Many communities have passed laws to outlaw abuses on cocoa farms, and the governments of Ghana, Mali, and the Ivory Coast have rescued some child slaves.

James Kofi Annan understands what these children are going through. He was six years old when his parents sold him. For seven years he was a slave. When he was thirteen, he managed to escape back to his parents' home.

He decided that he wanted to learn English and enrolled in school. He earned a university degree and found a good job in a bank. His passion, though, was to help children so they would not have to suffer the misery he had known. In 2003, he created the organization Challenging Heights, which is supported by the American organization Free the Slaves, and educates children so that they will know their rights and have the skills to escape poverty. Annan talks to parents about the importance of school and about the lasting damage caused by child labor. About 250 children aged four to fifteen are enrolled at his school. Some are former slaves, and others might have been sold into slavery if Challenging Heights hadn't reached them first.

In spite of these positive signs, much work remains. Some experts think thousands more children – and adults – remain as slaves on cocoa farms.

The Fight to End Slavery Today

People fight slavery today because they have been slaves themselves or because they have heard the stories of slaves. They are all united by a sense of outrage at the injustice of slavery.

Mauritania

Abdel Nasser Ould Yessa was born into a ruling class family in Mauritania, where his father was president of the Supreme Court. At the age of sixteen, Abdel already knew something was wrong in his country.

> In high school I read about the French Revolution. . . . The ideal . . . that "all men are born free and equal" captivated me. I began to see that what was happening in my country was not normal. I would come home from school and slaves would care for me. They would bring me drinks, wash my hands, massage my feet, and cook for me. . . . And one day I just said, "No!" If a slave came to care for me, I would refuse them. I started to do things myself. My mother was not happy, because, as she told me, "This is not noble." The slaves did not know how to react. They had never heard what I was saying: that all men are born free.

For more than eight hundred years, people have been born into slavery in Mauritania, a northwest African country with a population of only 3.1 million. The ruling class is made up of Arab-Berbers known as *bidanes*, "whites." The slaves are descended from the native black Africans. According to some estimates, over half a million people (a sixth of the population) live as slaves.

The *bidanes* believe that most forms of physical labor are degrading to them, and demand that slaves perform all the menial work. The economy of Mauritania rests entirely on the work of slaves like Bilal, who at age twenty works seven days a week. He rises before sunrise, eats a breakfast of rice or left-overs prepared by a slave woman, and drives his master's donkey cart to a well. There he fills two giant barrels of water by hand from a metal can and starts his rounds, delivering water to his master's customers. Working even when the sun is beating down at noon, he returns to the well seven or eight times every day, bringing about two hundred gallons (800 liters) of water to people who do not have running water. When the last of the water is delivered, he turns over the money to his master, and performs other exhausting chores until midnight.

Slave women clean, cook, and raise their masters' children. Their own children are sold away from them, and they themselves live in fear of being sexually abused.

In 1995, when Abdel Nasser Ould Yessa was living in Paris, he decided to change the lives of the slaves he had seen every day in his country. He joined with Mauritanian antislavery activist Boubacar Messaoud, the son of slaves, to form SOS Esclaves (SOS Slaves), an illegal organization that had to operate in secret.

Mauritania has passed antislavery laws four times since 1901, but none has been effective. In 2007, SOS Esclaves helped draft a law to penalize slaveholders. Anyone convicted of practicing slavery would serve up to ten years in jail, and anyone who promoted or defended it would also be punished. But the government has still not prosecuted any offenders, and the law does not permit human rights organizations to go to court on behalf of uneducated slaves to free them. Although much work remains to be done, SOS Esclaves won the 2009 Anti-Slavery Award from Anti-Slavery International for its groundbreaking efforts to wipe out slavery in Mauritania.

Lebanon

Beatrice Fernando lived in Sri Lanka with her three-year-old son. She hated to leave him, but she was poor and in desperate need of work. When an employment agency promised her a well-paying job in distant Lebanon, plus free room and board and airfare home, she agreed to leave her son with her parents and work there for two years as a housemaid.

On the plane ride she got her first hint that the job might not be what she expected. The man in the next seat warned her not to go. "Don't you know what happens to girls who go to Lebanon to work as maids? They're abused and raped, and some are even killed," he said. She did not listen.

At the employment agency in Lebanon, a man took her passport and made her stand in line with other women. "Lebanese men and women pace in front of us, examining our bodies as if we were vacuum cleaners," she later said. She would discover that that was all she was to her employer – a machine for cleaning.

CHILDREN HELPING CHILDREN

One morning in 1995, in Toronto, Canada, twelve-year-old Craig Kielburger was in the kitchen eating cereal when a front-page headline in the newspaper caught his eye: "Battled Child Labour, Boy, 12, Murdered. Defied members of 'carpet mafia.'"

A Pakistani boy his own age, Iqbal Masih, had worked unpaid at a loom for six long years, tying tiny knots to make carpets. Iqbal had been shot to death while riding his bike in the outskirts of the city of Lahore. The article ended, "Some believe his murder was carried out by angry members of the carpet industry who had made repeated threats to silence the young activist."

Who were the "carpet mafia," and why would they want to kill a twelve-year-old boy, Craig wondered. His curiosity opened his eyes to a whole new world, the world of child labor.

IQBAL'S STORY

Iqbal's family was poor and owed so much money that when their son was only four years old, they bonded him to the owner of a carpet factory for sixteen dollars. He slaved over a loom twelve or more hours a day, six days a week, to pay off his parents' debts. He was poorly fed. Sometimes his boss chained him to the loom, and frequently he beat him.

One day Iqbal ran away and came upon a rally where he heard members of an antislavery group explain that the Pakistani government had passed a law against debt labor, and had canceled all the debts that slave laborers owed their masters. The factory owners did not want anyone to know, because they wanted to continue paying low wages, and besides, nobody enforced the laws. The antislavery group helped to free Iqbal, and he began to speak publicly about his experiences.

Iqbal was only four feet two inches (under 130 cm) tall because of his years without good food, sunshine, and exercise. The sight of this tiny boy, almost hidden by

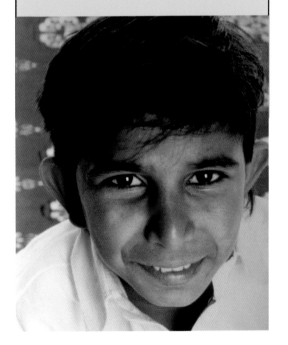

She was sent to work for a wealthy couple with three children who lived on the fourth floor of a luxury condominium. "My chores seem unending," she said. "I wash the windows, walls, and bathrooms. I shampoo carpets, polish floors and clean furniture. After twenty hours I am still not done." One morning, in despair, she woke up crying. Her mistress entered her room, took her brush from her hand, and began to strike her with it. "I give you shelter. I give you food. There is no reason for you to cry!" the woman yelled. After her employer left the apartment, Fernando tried to call the police for help, but the telephone was locked. She ran to the balcony to yell to someone on the street, but saw no one.

As the days passed, the beatings got worse. Fearful that her mistress would kill her, Fernando went to the balcony, looked down four floors, and jumped. She was not trying to kill herself. She only wanted to escape.

She survived the fall and awoke in the hospital. The doctors thought she would never walk again, but she did. With help from people at the hospital, she forced the employment agency to send her back home to Sri Lanka. Since gaining her freedom, she has worked with antislavery organizations and written a book, *In Contempt of Fate*, about her experience.

Human Trafficking

Beatrice Fernando was a victim of human trafficking. She took a huge chance in jumping off that balcony – but though her method of escape was unusual, her situation was not. People frequently leave poor, developing, or conflict-ridden countries for wealthier places in search of a better life. Many end up as victims of traffickers.

In 2008, the U.S. government estimated that as many as 800,000 people were being trafficked across international borders every year, and millions more within their own countries. Most of the victims of international trafficking are women and girls, and as many as half of them are children. Some end up as household slaves, and many others are forced to work as prostitutes.

Iqbal Masih, who was murdered in 1995 for opening the world's eyes to child slavery, received the first World's Children's Prize for the Rights of the Child after his death. At his funeral a young girl named Shenaz, who had worked in bonded labor making bricks, said, "The day Iqbal died, a thousand new Iqbals were born."

In 2000, U.S. president Bill Clinton signed a law called the Victims of Trafficking and Violence Act, saying, "This is slavery, plain and simple." The law made human trafficking illegal, and set severe penalties, including life imprisonment, for people who buy and sell human beings.

Human trafficking is not illegal everywhere. In Lebanon, Beatrice Fernando's employer had committed no crime. But in the United States, some people are paying the penalty.

United States

For centuries the United States has been a beacon for immigrants looking for a better life and a way out of poverty. Julia Gabriel was one of them. In 1992, when she was nineteen, she left Guatemala to find work in the United States. Her mother was earning only fifty-five dollars a month, and Julia wanted to help. But she could not enter the U.S. legally, so she arranged to be smuggled into the country.

She was in Arizona when she heard about a job in South Carolina. Two men, a Mexican and a Guatemalan, drove her and other workers in a crowded, dirty van across the country. For two days, they did not let them leave the van for food or even to use the toilet. As soon as they arrived in South Carolina, the men told the passengers that they had to pay the smuggling fee – the cost of transportation. As the days went by, the crew leader and his associates also charged them for rent, meager amounts of food, and showers – a debt they would have to repay by working. The workers were watched by armed guards, and were told that anyone who tried to escape would be killed.

They lived in a large compound. "If someone even just tried to attempt to walk out of the place, they'd beat them," Gabriel said. "They would constantly taunt us and shoot guns up in the air as a way to intimidate us and would say things like 'we own you,' and 'you should be grateful to even be in this country.'"

Gabriel's workday started at four a.m., when she was roused by the sound of gunshots. She harvested cucumbers seven days a week for twelve hours a day. After the bosses subtracted the money they claimed she owed from her wages, she was paid just twenty dollars a week – about twenty-four cents an hour.

One day the bosses overheard one of the workers say, "In the U.S., you don't have to work by force." They turned on him, ruthlessly beating him and a co-worker who tried to help him. They even shot a worker who wanted to leave.

a microphone, speaking out courageously for children's rights helped rouse public outrage throughout the world, and Iqbal won the Reebok Human Rights Youth in Action Award. When he went to the United States to receive his award in 1994, he held up a carpet tool. This was what his owner had used to beat children who did something wrong, he explained.

Unfortunately, the owner of the business where I worked told us that it is America who asks us to enslave the children. American people like the cheap carpets, the rugs, and the towels that we make. So they want bonded labor to go on. I appeal to you that you stop people from using children as bonded laborers because the children need to use a pen rather than the instruments of child labor.

Many people suspect that Iqbal was killed by the "carpet mafia" – thugs employed by Pakistani carpet factories – because his message was getting through, and turning people's hearts against manufacturers who abused children in their factories.

CRAIG'S STORY

Iqbal's story enraged Craig Kielburger. The more he learned about child labor and child slavery, the more determined he became to fight it.

Craig started a club at his school, and it quickly grew into an organization named Free the Children. First, he and his friends set out to learn as much as they could about child labor. From the International Labor Organization, for example, they learned that there were about 250 million working children in the world. The next step was to educate other children, so they made presentations in schools and encouraged children to write to companies or government leaders about the issue.

Free the Children (FTC) has grown, but its focus remains the same: getting young people in the richest countries in the world to support young people in the poorest. Its young volunteers speak in schools and encourage children to raise money to help free other children overseas. FTC's volunteers also spend time in poor villages, and they have figured out practical ways of wiping out child slavery. For example, in Leiwing, China, FTC got fathers involved in building a school. When parents felt they needed their children to work in the fields, FTC gave the families piglets, which could be raised for more income. Now, with the prospect of more money for the families, 98 percent of the village's children go to school.

After three months, Gabriel escaped in the middle of the night and found work on a tomato farm three hours away. There, she said, she was "making only enough to get by, but we were free, no one beat us, and we could go to the store or the Laundromat whenever we wanted to."

While she was on that farm, speakers from the Coalition of Immokalee Workers, a group that promotes fair treatment of farm laborers, came to tell the laborers about their rights. (Immokalee, which rhymes with "broccoli," is the name of a town in Florida where many immigrant farm workers are employed.) Gabriel told them her story, and together they began to pressure the U.S. government to look into the conditions she reported.

The U.S. Department of Justice and the Coalition learned that Gabriel's old bosses had enslaved more than four hundred people in Florida, South Carolina, and Georgia. The government charged the bosses with enslavement and other crimes, and the case went to court in 1997. Gabriel told the judge, "Do not show compassion to these men, for they showed no compassion to those who were under their care." The two men were given a stiff sentence – fifteen years in prison – for holding migrant laborers as slaves and forcing them to work against their will.

Julia Gabriel now works in the United States legally, and continues to help the Coalition, which informs workers of their rights and helps bring human traffickers to trial. Since 1997, the Coalition has helped free more than a thousand farm workers, and has seen more than a dozen employers convicted of criminal acts.

The Coalition has organized boycotts of fast-food restaurants that cannot guarantee that their tomatoes were picked by free workers, and many young people have helped with their campaigns. Now, some grocery stores and restaurants will only buy produce grown on farms where workers are well treated.

Many farm workers still face intimidation, mistreatment, and terror, but the FBI now actively enforces the law against human trafficking. When slave owners are behind bars, they cannot hurt honest workers.

TO BE FREE

Little has changed for slaves since long ago. Like the ancient Sumerians who sold their children to get out of debt, James Kofi Annan's parents in Ghana sold him. Just as slave women in Ancient Rome had never-ending household tasks, Beatrice Fernando worked almost around the clock in Lebanon. Like the ninth-century Zanj, transported from East Africa to work the salt marshes of Iraq, Julia Gabriel was trafficked from Arizona to the cucumber fields of South Carolina. Cotton pickers like Solomon Northup suffered beatings in the American South just as Amadou did when he picked cocoa beans in the Ivory Coast. And Patricius – later Saint Patrick – herded sheep in ancient Ireland just as Giemma's young slave Francis herded goats, sheep, cows, and camels.

Do You Remember Francis?

The Francis you read about at the start of this book was Francis Bok, who lived with his family in Sudan until Giemma carried him off into slavery. He was determined to get back to his parents, and one day when he was fourteen he left the cows to graze in the forest and fled to the main road. His freedom lasted only twenty minutes, until a man on horseback spotted him and returned him to Giemma, who beat him with a cattle whip and made him promise not to run away again. But nothing would stop Francis. Two days later he tried again. He took the cows to graze and waited for sunset to escape through the woods. Again he didn't get far. When he stopped for water at a river, he saw Giemma. At home, his master bound his hands and feet so tightly with rawhide that they swelled and bled. Giemma's wife wanted him dead and kept repeating, "Why don't you kill him?" But Giemma did not want to lose a good cowherd. Again Francis promised not to escape, and again Giemma believed him. It did not take many days before Francis realized that he would break that promise, but he decided to give himself time.

When Francis was seventeen, tall and strong and with a better idea of how to flee undetected, he left with the cows early one morning. As soon as they started to graze, he ran deep into the woods. He ran for hours, until he reached a market town. He went to the police, but instead of helping him they made him their kitchen boy without pay. He escaped again, and this time met a kind truck driver who sheltered him for months and gave him bus fare to the capital, Khartoum.

From there Francis reached a refugee camp, where he met people from his hometown. With their help, he got a forged passport and passage to Egypt.

Two years after his escape from Giemma, the United States opened its doors to Francis, and in August 1999, he began his new life in North Dakota, a place he'd never heard of.

Francis relished his freedom. For the first time in his life, he got paid for his work. He began to save money for school, he had friends, and he said "yes" when he wanted and "no" when he wanted. What a difference from being a slave!

Less than a year after arriving in America, Francis got a call from Jesse Sage of the American Anti-Slavery Group (AASG), a modern-day abolitionist organization. Would Francis work for them, telling his story? He wasn't sure. He'd been through a lot, and he didn't want to leave his new home. But when he saw pictures of former slaves from Sudan, some scarred and mutilated by their masters and others smiling after their rescue by the AASG, he remembered his father's words, "You are like twelve men" – *muycharko* – and he knew what his father would have wanted.

Though reliving the past is painful, Francis agreed to do it. He has spoken to the U.S. Congress and the United Nations about slavery in Sudan, and has written a book, *Escape from Slavery*, about his experiences. "I used to lie awake at night and wonder who will come to free me," he says, "and so I am actually dedicating my life experience on behalf of millions around the world who cannot speak for themselves." Francis's parents did not survive the raid in which he was captured, but he has returned to visit his village, where he is working with a charity to build a school.

How Can I Help?

To wipe out slavery, governments, businesses, and ordinary people have to work together. What can you do?

Ask questions. When you ask, "Who picked the tomatoes we're buying for our sandwiches? Were they free laborers or slaves?" you are putting pressure on businesses.

Look for labels like "Fair Trade" or "GoodWeave." These show that antislavery organizations have inspected the farms and factories and found free laborers at work. Consumers can let merchants know that slave-free products are good business.

Ask the government to do its part. Every government can pass tough antislavery laws to make sure that slave-made products don't enter its country. Governments can teach police to spot signs that someone may be a slave, and require them to enforce antislavery laws.

Learn and teach. Since many people think slavery ended long ago, a good way to start abolishing it is by educating people about slavery in today's world. Students and community groups can invite guest speakers from antislavery organizations, and help to raise funds for these groups. That money supports antislavery workers in poor countries, helping them free slaves and bonded laborers.

Many other ideas are listed on the websites of antislavery organizations. Here are some to get you started:

American Anti-Slavery Group, www.iabolish.org
Anti-Slavery International, www.antislavery.org
Free the Children, www.freethechildren.com
Free the Slaves, www.freetheslaves.net

TIME LINE

Dates in coloured bars indicate time periods.
Dates below bars indicate world events.

BCE   **2700–2200: Egyptian Old Kingdom**   **880–860: Assyrian King Ashurnasirpal II rebuilds Nimrud**

3000: Rise of Sumerian cities   776: Greece holds first Olympics
1790: Law Code of Babylonian King Hammurabi
1200: Exodus of Hebrews from Egypt

622–712: Birth and early expansion of Islam to east and west
    650–1900: About 12 million Africans sent out of Sahara and East Africa into slavery

793: Vikings attack Lindisfarne
869: Revolt of Zanj slaves in Iraq
1212: Children's Crusades
1260: Mamluks stop Mongol invasion of Egypt
1348: Black Death strikes Europe
1400: Islam established in Malaya and Sumatra
1450: Portuguese–West African slave trade under way
1492: Christopher Columbus lands in Bahamas

18th century: European Enlightenment   **19th century: Caliphate of Sokoto (Africa) [1812–1890s]**
Mid-18th century: Caribbean sugar production surges [1730s to 1780s]
1770–1870: Iranun and Balangingi slave trade
1787–1838: British abolition movement

1776: American Declaration of Independence   1803: Louisiana Purchase
1789: French Revolution begins   1804: Haiti proclaims independence
                  1807: British Parliament passes bill abolishing slave trade

6th–5th century: Buddhist religion begins   *CE*   ⟶

146: Romans conquer Greece   117: Height of Roman Empire

73: Spartacus leads slave revolt   406: Patricius (St. Patrick) enslaved

1500–1870: At least 12 million Africans shipped to the Americas

1520–66: Ottoman Empire reaches greatest extent

Late 16th century: Laws restrict Russian serfs [1580s–1590s]   ⟶

Early 1640s: French introduce slavery to Martinique

1602: Dutch East India Company established

1619: First African slaves arrive in America

1693: Gold discovered in Brazil

1830s–80s: Reform Period, Ottoman Empire   1930s: Stalin establishes Soviet gulag

1833–1861: Height of American abolitionism   1939–45: World War II—Nazi slave labor camps

Mid-1800s: Height of blackbirding in southern Pacific [mid-1840s to 1880s]   Early 1950s: Laogai camps set up in China

1831: Slave revolts in Virginia and Jamaica

1838: Britain frees 800,000 slaves in West Indies

1850: U.S. Congress passes Fugitive Slave Act

1863: Lincoln issues Emancipation Proclamation

1865: U.S. government abolishes slavery

1995: Child anti-slavery campaigner Iqbal Masih murdered

2001: Cocoa Protocol signed by chocolate companies and U.S. Congressmen

SOURCES

Hundreds of books, articles, and websites educated us as we researched slavery. Here, we list only those we consulted most frequently. A complete bibliography is available at our website, www.fivethousandyearsofslavery.com.

Several reference works deserve special mention for providing background and guiding us to research by specialists: *A Historical Guide to World Slavery*, edited by Seymour Drescher and Stanley L. Engerman (New York: Oxford University Press, 1998); *Macmillan Encyclopedia of World Slavery*, vols. 1 and 2, edited by Paul Finkelman and Joseph C. Miller (New York: Simon & Schuster Macmillan, 1998); and *Chronology of World Slavery*, by Junius P. Rodriguez (Santa Barbara, CA: ABC-CLIO, 1999). *Inhuman Bondage: The Rise and Fall of Slavery in the New World*, by the great slavery scholar David Brion Davis, gave us perspective on slavery throughout history and on the birth of abolitionism. We consulted works by many of the major scholars of American and world slavery (Ira Berlin, Moses I. Finley, Henry Louis Gates Jr., Eugene D. Genovese, James Oliver Horton and Lois E. Horton, Herbert S. Klein, Bernard Lewis, Orlando Patterson, James Walvin, and James Francis Warren, to name only a few). We also referred to the websites Documenting the American South, sponsored by the University Library at the University of North Carolina at Chapel Hill and accessible at http://docsouth.unc.edu, and *Born in Slavery: Slave Narratives from the Federal Writers' Project, 1936–1938*, available at the Library of Congress website, http://memory.loc.gov.

The Trans-Atlantic Slave Trade Database, sponsored by Emory University and several partners, at http://www.slavevoyages.org/tast/index.faces, was our source for statistics on slave shipments from Africa to Europe, North America, and South America. We used figures from the Estimates database, which are higher than the documented figures and come closer to the probable totals.

For images of slaves in Africa and the Americas, we referred frequently to The Atlantic Slave Trade and Slave Life in the Americas: A Visual Record, a website compiled by Jerome S. Handler and Michael L. Tuite Jr. A project of the Virginia Foundation for the Humanities and the University of Virginia Library, it is accessible at http://hitchcock.itc.virginia.edu/Slavery/index.php.

PHOTO SOURCES

Page 4: *Standard of Ur,* "War" © The Trustees of the British Museum. **Page 7:** *Head of a Prisoner.* Courtesy of the Saint Louis Art Museum. **Page 8:** *Hagar and the Angel in the Desert* by James Tissot. Courtesy of The Jewish Museum, NY / Art Resource, NY. **Page 9:** *Hebrews building cities.* Courtesy of Eric Lessing / Art Resource, NY. **Page 11:** *Mosaic with circus scene: fighting with leopards.* Courtesy of Snark / Art Resource, NY. **Page 12:** *Sparticus's Death* by Hermann Vogel. Courtesy of the Picture Collection, New York Public Library. **Page 17:** *Pompeiian ladies with their slave hairdresser.* Courtesy of the Schomberg Center / Art Resource, NY. **Page 18:** *Two-handled jar* © 2011 by the Museum of Fine Arts, Boston. **Page 21:** *Statue of Saint Patrick* © 2003 by Bernd Biege. **Page 27:** *Burying plague victims of Tournai.* From Annals of Gilles de Muisit. Courtesy of Snark / Art Resource, NY. **Page 29:** *Catherine, the Mulatto Woman.* Courtesy of Scala / Ministero per I Beni e le Attivita culturali / Art Resource, NY. **Page 31:** *Supplice du Grand Knout.* From *Voyage en Siberie* by Jean Chappe D'Auteroche & Stepan Petrovič, pg. 371. 1770. **Page 33:** *Mihrasb and Tahrusiyye watching Darab fighting the Zanjis.* From *Race and Slavery in the Middle East* by Bernard Lewis, pg. 24. 1580-1585. **Page 36:** *Slave Market of Cairo.* Courtesy of the Library of Congress. **Page 37:** *Christian Slavery in Barbary.* Courtesy of Schomburg Center / Art Resource, NY. **Page 38:** *Slavery in Zanzibar* © National Maritime Museum, Greenwich, London. **Page 40:** *Slaves taken from a Dhow captured by HMS* Undine. Courtesy of the Library of Congress. **Page 46:** *Funerary Carving of African in European Dress* © National Maritime Museum, Greenwich, London. **Page 48:** *Enslaved Africans transported by canoe, Congo, 1880s.* Courtesy of Making of America Collection, Cornell University. **Page 49:** *Two mutilated children.* Courtesy of http://revcom.us/i/172/Amputated_Congolese_youth.jpg. **Page 52:** *Landing of Columbus.* Courtesy of the Library of Congress. **Page 55:** *Sacrificial offering.* Courtesy of the Library of Congress. **Page 59:** *Bartolomé de la Casas* by Constantino Brumidi. Courtesy of the Architect of the Capitol, Washington, DC. **Page 61:** Mahommah Baquaqua article. Courtesy of the New York Public Library. **Page 65:** *Slavery/Shipboard Scene.* Courtesy of Mary Evans Picture Library. **Page 67:** *Porters d'Eau.* Courtesy of the Library of Congress. **Page 69:** *Chatiments Domestiques.* Courtesy of the Library of Congress. **Page 73:** *Treadmill Scene in Jamaica.* Courtesy of the Library of Congress. **Page 75:** *Spiritual Healer.* Courtesy of the John Carter Brown Library, Brown University, Rhode Island. **Page 76:** *The Celebrated Graman Quacy.* Courtesy of the John Carter Brown Library, Brown University, Rhode Island. **Page 77:** *Granville Sharp.* Courtesy of the Library of Congress. **Page 80:** *Thomas Clarkson.* Courtesy of the Wisbech and Fenland Museum, Cambridge, UK. **Page 82:** *Diagram of slave ship* Brookes. Courtesy of the Library of Congress. **Page 84:** *Anti-Slavery Medallion by Josiah Wedgwood, c. 1787* © The Trustees of the British Museum; Photo courtesy of Uncle Tom's Cabin Historic Site. **Page 85:** *Sugar basins advert.* Courtesy of The Religious Society of Friends in Britain. **Page 86:** *Phillis Wheatley.* Courtesy of the Library of Congress. **Page 87:** *Slave with Iron Muzzle.* Courtesy of Hill Collection of Pacific Voyages, University of California, San Diego. **Page 87:** *Gustavus Vassa.* Courtesy of the New York Public Library. **Page 88:** *Toussaint L'Ouverture.* Courtesy of the Library of Congress. **Page 95:** *Landing Negroes at Jamestown.* Courtesy of the Library of Congress. **Page 97:** *Gravestone of Venture Smith* © Eric Rennie. **Page 98:** *"To be sold" sign.* Courtesy of the Library of Congress. **Page 100:** *Band of the Jaw-Bone John-Canoe.* Courtesy of the Yale Center for British Art / Paul Mellon Collection. **Page 102:** *The Life of George Washington – the Farmer* by Junius Stearns. Courtesy of the Library of Congress. **Page 103:** *Black-and-white revolutionary soldiers.* From http://americanrevolution.org/blk.html. **Page 110:** *The Horrid Massacre.* Courtesy of the Library of Congress. **Page 114:** *Joseph Cinquez article.* Courtesy of the Library of Congress. **Page 115:** *Frederick Douglass.* Courtesy of the Library of Congress. **Page 116:** *Sojourner Truth.* Courtesy of the Library of Congress. **Page 119:** *Uncle Tom's Cabin Jigsaw Puzzle.* Courtesy of Mary Schlosser, collector. **Page 120:** *The Resurrection of Henry "Box" Brown.* Courtesy of the Library of Congress. **Page 123:** *Harriet Tubman.* Courtesy of the Library of Congress. **Page 125:** *Harpers Ferry Insurrection.* Courtesy of the Library of Congress. **Page 126:** *Recruitment poster.* Courtesy of the Library of Congress. **Page 135:** *Balangingi garay.* Rafael Mouleon, Construccion Navales: bajo un aspecto artistico por el restangador del Museo Naval, Catalogo descriptivo dos tomos. 3 vols. Madrid, 1890. **Page 136:** *Iranun Warrior.* Frank Marryat, *Borneo and the Indian Archipelago,* 1848. **Page 138:** *South Sea islanders on the deck of a ship arriving at Bundaberg, 1895.* Courtesy of the State Library of Queensland. **Page 141:** *Mui-Tsai.* Courtesy of Anti-Slavery International, London. **Page 145:** *Gut Parka: Fishing from kayak,* 1872. Courtesy of the Alaska Native Collection, Smithsonian National Museum of Natural History. **Page 146:** *Prisoners work at Belbaltlag, a Soviet Gulag camp.* Courtesy of Central Russian Film and Photo Archive. **Page 147:** *Prisoner from a Nazi slave labor camp.* Courtesy of the Library of Congress. **Page 150:** *Mark Kwadwo On Lake Volta in Ghana* by Joao Silva © The New York Times. **Page 154:** *Iqbal Masih.* Courtesy of Corbis Canada.

INDEX

Page numbers in italics are references to sidebars and captions.

abolitionism
in Ancient Israel, 10
in Britain, 78–93
in St-Domingue (Haiti), 87–88
in United States, 111–124
modern, 145, 147–148, 149, 150–151, *151,* 153-156, *153–156,* 157–158
Adams, John Quincy, 114–115
Africa
export of slaves from, 34–36, *36,* 46,–47, 61–65
slavery in, *34–35,* 43–46, *47,* 47–50, *49, 50–51*
Akkad, 3–4
Aleutian Islands, *see* Pribilof Islands
Al-Yaqubi, 43
American Revolution, 101–103
Amistad, 113–115
Annan, James Kofi, *151*
Anskar, Saint, 23
anti-slavery organizations
American Anti-Slavery Group, 158, 159
American Anti-Slavery Society, 112, 115
Anti-Slavery International, 153, 159
Coalition of Immokalee Workers, 156
Free the Children, *156,* 159
Free the Slaves, 159
Society for Effecting the Abolition of the Slave Trade, 80
SOS Esclaves, 153
Assyria, 3–5
Auld, Hugh and Sophia, 109
Australia, 137, *138,* 139
Aztecs, 54, *55*

Babylonia, 4–5
Bailey, Frederick, *see* Douglass, Frederick
Balangingi, 133–136
Ball, Charles, 94
Baquaqua, Mahommah Gardo, 61, 66

Barbary Coast, *34–35*
Beah, Ishmael, 149
Belgium, *49*
Benezet, Anthony, *81*
Bible, Hebrew, 7–10, 33, 85, *92,* 100–101, 109
Birkett, Mary, 85
blackbirding 137–139
Blackburn, Thornton and Lucie, 119–120
Bok, Francis 1–2, 157–158
Borneo, 134
Brazil 53, 66, 67, *67, 69,* 71, 74, 75
Broteer, *see* Smith, Venture
Brown, John, *see* revolts, trials
Brown, William Wells, 96, 108
Buddhism, 129–130
Buk, Francis, *see* Bok, Francis

Caesar, Julius, 15
Canada, 66, 104, 118–120
Carleton, Sir Guy, 103
Catholic Church, 21–23, *23,* 26, *27–28,* 28, 29, 58, 59, 66
child soldiers, 149–150
Child Soldiers Protocol, 149–150
Children's Crusade, *27–28*
China, 131, 134, 140–143, *143,* 147–148
chocolate, *see* cocoa
Christian slaves
Barbary Coast, *34–35*
boy soldiers, 39
Middle Ages, 26–27
Christianity, 33, 80–81, *92,* 100–101, 108–109
Cinqué, 113–115
civil rights, U.S., 127–128
Civil War, American, 124–127
Clarkson, Thomas, 79–81, *80,* 83–85, 89, 90, 93
cocoa, 150–152
International Cocoa Initiative, 151
Coffin, Levi and Catherine, 121
Columbus, Christopher, 52–53, *52,* 58
Congo, *48, 49*

Constitution, United States, 104, 116, 127
coolies, *138–139*
cotton
    gin, *105*
    in Africa, 39
    in United States, 105–108
Cuba, 148–149
Cugoano, Ottobah, *86*

Datini, Francesco, 27–29
Declaration of Independence, United States, 101, 115
Demerara (Guyana), 91–92
Denmark, *see* Scandinavia
Dessalles, Pierre, 67–68, 70
Douglass, Frederick, 109, *115,* 115–116, 126–127
Dunmore, Lord, 102–103
Dutch East India Company, 133

Egypt, Ancient, 6–8, *7*
emancipation
    in British West Indies, 93
    in Haiti (St-Domingue), 87–89
    in United States, 126–127
encomienda, 59
Enlightenment, *92*
Equiano, Olaudah, *86–87, 87*
Ethiopia, 35, 37, 48, 130
Exodus from Egypt, 8, *9,* 33, 109

Fadlan, Ahmad ibn, 25
Falconbridge, Alexander, 83–84
Falun Gong, 147–148
Fernando, Beatrice, 153–154
Fiji, 137, 138–139
Foss, John, *34–35*
Freeman, Elizabeth, 104
French Revolution, 87–89, 152
Fugitive Slave Act of 1850, 117–118

Gabriel, Julia, 155–156
Garrison, William Lloyd, 111–112, 115–116, 124
Germany, 146–147
Ghana 96, *150–151,* 151
Gilgamesh, 3
gladiators, 11, *11–12*
Grandy, Charles, 108
Greece, Ancient, 11–20
gulag, 146
Gullah, *99*

Haiti, *see* St-Domingue
Hammurabi, Code of, 5
Harpers Ferry, 123–124, *125*
Hawaii, 137
Henry, Patrick, 102
Henry, Prince, the Navigator, 46
Heyrick, Elizabeth, 90
Hinduism, 130
human sacrifice, 25–26, 45–46, 53–54, *55,* 57, 136
human trafficking, 151, 154–155
Hunt, Richard and Jane, *118*

Ibn Battuta, 43
indentured servants, 94–95
India, 129–130
Indonesia, 131, 134
Iranun, *134,* 134–136
Iroquois, 57–58
Islam, 33–41
    in Southeast Asia, 132
Israel, Ancient, 7–10
Italy, 26–30
Ivory Coast, 151

Jackson, Andrew, 105–106
Jacobs, Harriet, 99–100, 110, 117–118
Jamaica, 68, 70, 74, 92–93
Jefferson, Thomas, 102
Jewitt, John R., *56*

jihad, 34, 48
John Canoe, 99–100, *100*
Johnson, Anthony, 94–95, 98
just war, 58

Kali, 130
Kansas-Nebraska Act, 123
Kielberger, Craig, *153–156*
King, Boston, 103–104

Las Casas, Bartolomé de, *59,* 59–60,
Laws
    Ancient Greece and Rome, 18–19
    British colonial in China 142
    Code Noir, 71–72
    Italy, 28–29
    Pacific islands, 139
    South America and Caribbean, 71–73
    under Islam, 33–34, 35, 39–40, 41
    United States (*see also* laws by name), 98–99, 117–118, 122, 127
    Vikings, 24
"Lay of the Rig," 23–24
Lebanon, 153–154
Leopold II, King, 49
Lim, Janet, 140–142
Lincoln, Abraham, 117, 124, 126–127
Long, Edward, 68
Louisiana Purchase, 105
Lu, Sam, 147–148

Malay Peninsula, 132
Mali, 46, 96, 150–151
Mamluks, 39
Mansfield, Lord Chief Justice, 79
manumission (acquiring freedom), laws of
    Ancient Greece and Rome, 19–20
    Islam, 34
    Italy, 28–30
    Scandinavia, 24–25
    South America and the Caribbean, 74–75

maps
    Africa, 42
    Ancient Near East, 5
    Asia and the Southern Pacific, 131
    Atlantic Slave Trade, 62
    Islamic World, 35
    Roman Empire, 14
    United States during the Civil War, 106
maroons, 75, 77, 98
Martin, Fredericka, 145
Martinique, 67–68, 71
Masih, Iqbal, *153–155*
Mauritania, 41, 152–153
Meli, 50–51
Mesopotamia, 3
Messaoud, Boubacar, 153
Middle Ages, 21–31
Middle Passage, 61, 84
mining
    Ancient Greece and Rome, 17–18
    Egyptian Nubia and Sahara, 38
    Hispaniola, 58
    South America, 71, *139*
    United States, 128
Missouri Compromise, 107
More, Hannah, 87
Mott, Lucretia B., *118*
Muhammad, Prophet, 33–34, 35–36
Muhammad, Ali ibn, 32–33
mui-tsai, 140–143, *143*
Mwachitete, Msatulwa, 45–46

Napoleon, 89
Native Americans
    enslavement of, 53, 58–60, *60*
    slavery practiced by, 53–58, *56*
Nazis, 146–147, *147*
Netherlands, 75, *76*
New Hebrides, 137, 138
New Zealand, 137, 139

newspapers, anti-slavery
  Frederick Douglass's Paper, 116
  Freedom's Journal, 111
  The Liberator, 111, 124
  The North Star, 116
Nigeria, 46, 48
Nootka, 5–57, *56*
North Korea, 148
Northup, Solomon, 107, *108*
Norway, *see* Scandinavia

Old Calabar, 46–47, *63–64*
Otis, James, Jr., 102
Ottoman Empire, 39–40

Pakistan, *153–155*
Patrick, Saint (Patricius), 21–22
paybringers, 18
Pennsylvania Hall, 113
Philemon, 15
Philippines, 131, 134
Pieters, C. Z., 133–137
plague, 26, *26*
Portugal, 46, 63
potlatch, 57
Pribilof Islands, 144–145
Prince, Mary, *68–69*

Quakers, 80, *80–81,* 85, 95, 112
Quassie, Graman, *76*
quilombo, 75
Qur'an, 33–36

Ramsay, James, 80
Revolts, in the U.S.
  Brown, John, 123–124, *125*
  New York, 98
  Prosser, Gabriel, 105
  Stono, 98
  Turner, Nat, 109–110, *110*

rice, 97
Roberts, James, 105–106
Robin John, Ancona Robin and Little Ephraim, *63–64*
Rome, Ancient, 11–20
runaway slaves, 5, 19, 29, 45–46, 74–75, 77, 98, 99, 103, 118–122, *120*
Russia, *30–31,* 144–145

St-Domingue (Haiti), 87–89, *88*
San, 44, 48
Scandinavia, 22–26
Scott, Dred and Harriet Robinson, 122
serfs, *30–31*
Sewall, Samuel, 100–101
Sharp, Granville, *78,* 78–79, 80, *86*
Sharp, William, 78
Sharpe, Samuel, 92
ships, slave
  Brookes, 82
  Carl, 137
  Daphne, 138–139
  Petronella, 133–135
  Polly, 34
  Zong, 65, *86*
Sibell, 63
Sierra Leone, 104, 115, 149
Simcoe, John Graves, 118
slave, defined, 2, *22*
slave culture in the Americas, African influence on
  entertainment, 99–100
  housing, 99
  language, *99*
  religion, 73–74
slave labor camps and prisons
  China (*laogai*), 147–148
  Cuba, 148–149
  Soviet (gulag), 146
  Nazi, 146–147
  North Korea, 148
  United States, 127–128

slave trade
    Atlantic, 46–47 61–65, *95,* 95–96
    East African, 34–35, *36, 41*
    Southern Pacific, 137–139
    Sulu Archipelago, 133–137
    Trans-Saharan, 34–35, *36, 43*
smallpox, *53*
Smalls, Robert, 125–126
Smith, Venture, 95–97, *97*
Sokoto, 44, 48
Solzhenitsyn, Alexander, 146
Somerset, James, 79
Southeast Asia, 131–137
Spartacus, 11–13
Spartans, *14*
Stanton, Elizabeth Cady, *118*
Stedman, John Gabriel, 69–70, 72–73, *76*
Strong, Jonathan, 78–79
Sudan, 2, *39,* 40, 41, 157–158
sugar
    boycott, 85
    production, 67–70
Sulu Archipelago, 133–137
Sumer, 3-4
Surinam, 69–70, 72–73, *76*
Sweden, *see* Scandinavia

Tahiti, 137
Taino, 53, *53*
Taney, Roger B., 122
Tanganyika, Lake, 36
Tappan, Lewis, 113–115
Tippu Tip, *36*
Tlingit, 54–55
Toussaint L'Ouverture, 88, *88*
trials
    Amistad, 113–115
    blackbirding, 138–139
    Brown, John, 123–124
    Freeman, Elizabeth, 104

    human trafficking, 156
    Scott, Dred, 122
    Somerset, James, 79
    Stono, 98
triangle trade, 61
Truth, Sojourner, *116,* 116–117
Tswana, 44, 48
Tubman, Harriet, 121–122, *122*
Tupinamba, 53–54
Turkey *see* Ottoman Empire
Tuscarora, 57
Tye, Colonel, 103

Uganda, 149
Uncle Tom's Cabin, 119
Underground Railroad, 120–121–122
Union of Soviet Socialist Republics, 146
United Nations, 149–150

Vassa, Gustavus, *see* Equiano, Olaudah
Vikings, 22–26

Walker, David, 111
War of 1812, 105–106
Washington, George, 101, *102,* 104
Wedgwood, Josiah, *84*
Weld, Angelina Grimké 112–113
Wheatley, Phillis, 86, *86*
Wilberforce, William, 81, 87, 91, 93
Williams, George Washington, 49
Women
    abolitionists, 85–87, 86, 90–91, 112–113, 116–118, 121–122
    women's rights, *118*

Yessa, Abdel Nasser Ould, 152–153

Zambia, *50*
Zanj, 32–33, *33,* 38
Zanzibar, *36,* 38, *38, 41*